# of arcs and circles

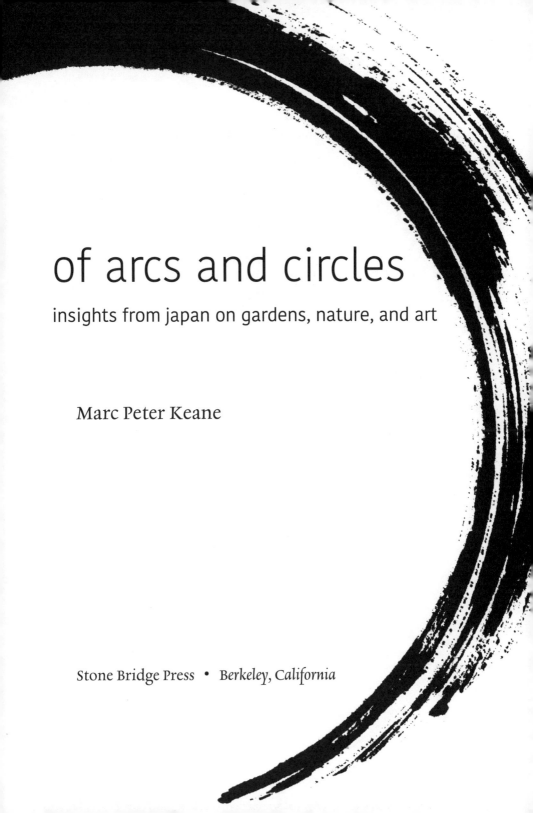

# of arcs and circles

insights from japan on gardens, nature, and art

Marc Peter Keane

Stone Bridge Press • Berkeley, California

Published by
Stone Bridge Press
P. O. Box 8208, Berkeley, CA 94707
TEL 510-524-8732 • sbp@stonebridge.com • www.stonebridge.com

Printed in the United States of America.

First print edition, 2022.

p-ISBN 978-1-61172-072-3
e-ISBN 978-1-61172-954-2

contents

of arcs and circles

Here is my secret. It's quite simple:
One sees clearly only with the heart.
Anything essential is invisible to the eyes.

Antoine de Saint-Exupéry
1943, The Little Prince

magnitudes

Coming to terms with, and finding one's place within, the vastness of the world

---

I live in a city, in a small wooden house on the edge of the hustle and press where the streets narrow and quickly rise from flat-land into forested hills. I share it with a million and a half other people. The city, not the house. We meet from time to time. Some of us. On the street. In trains. On hot summer evenings at festivals, dressed in light cotton *yukata*, fanning away our sweat, strolling in a crush down narrow streets. I've never met them all. I pray I never do. I think if I were to do that—to somehow meet a million and a half people—just like that, all at once, out of the blue, on some broad avenue or along the banks of one of the rivers that course through the city, the enormity of the moment would kill me. Just like that. Like looking on the face of the Creator, and knowing what is forbidden.

We know nothing of magnitudes.

Even if they were all placid, all million and a half of them, inwardly turned, expressionless, the way people are on trains, even then or maybe especially then, the magnitude would be unbearable. The faces of those in front looking quietly this way and that. Beyond them, a sea of heads receding back through the landscape until they disappear beyond the horizon.

A million and a half heads. I figured it out once. Shoulder to shoulder, that many people would cover sixty acres. I don't suppose anyone can ever know that sort of thing for certain, but the number sticks with me. Sixty acres of people, on-their-way-to-work-sleepy, on-their-way-home-tired. Just milling around. Mute.

Yes, I'm sure. I'd die on the spot.

They wouldn't have to be an angry mob, armed with sticks, charging about violently. No, the terror's not in that. It's simply the reality of the magnitude, of coming face to face with what a-million-and-a-half means. That alone would do it.

We know nothing of magnitudes. Not least our own.

We cannot even conceive the edge of its form, let alone its breadth or height. World population eight billion? Just words and far too easy to speak. Too smooth, too glib to truly express the scope of what they encompass. The words that mean that number should be longer. They should take an hour to say. They should take a week. Months. If the words took months to say then, having spoken nonstop for days on end, out of breath, fatigued beyond sensibility like a marathon monk who has run his way through mountains and cities to another plane of understanding, then in some small way the concept *eight billion* might flow naturally from the words.

In order to say "eight billion people" you should have to enunciate eight billion names—first name, last name, everything—the whole shebang. One after another, on and on into night, day after day. Then, and only then, could you approach some sense of what eight billion people actually represents.

The fastest speakers in the world can rattle off around 650 words a minute. Streaming twenty-four-seven, it would still take one of them seventeen years just to recite our first names. Just the *first* names. Even if a machine were brought to the task, clicking off 600,000 names a minute to get the job done in a week, even then the understanding of having actually said the names would be tempered by the stunning realization that in the seven days it took to voice them, a million of the named would have died. Nearly three million more would have been born.

We cannot even speak quickly enough to name the dead, let alone the living. We do not know. Not our names, not our numbers, certainly not the magnitudes of our own world.

•

Several years ago, I had a strange experience flying into New York. It could have been any city I suppose, I'm not sure it would make a difference, but it was New York. I remember that for sure. We were still many miles out, traveling at several hundred miles an hour. It was dusk and the sky was beginning to darken and tint with twilight colors. Pastel bands of light flowed over the airplane's silver wing the way a sunset melts into a calm lake.

As we approached the city, the plane descended through a layer of clouds, and for a while we were shrouded in a gray-white light. Easing out from the bottom of the clouds, we could see below us low, rolling hills covered with dark forest. Among the trees was a web of narrow roads, and dotted along those roads were houses in small clearings. Inside the windows of each house, evening lights were being lit and I imagined that I could just make out what was going on inside. A family sitting down to dinner. A couple hugging. A boy with his dog watching TV. Each house, each lit window, a story.

As we approached the city, the trees began to give way to more houses, then housing developments, then apartment buildings, the structures increasing in size as the population grew in concentration, rising steadily and unceasingly toward the nucleus of Manhattan. And in each of those houses, and in all of those housing developments, and in every apartment building, evening lights were being lit, and the stories began to pile up within my brain faster than I could make sense of them. A plate thrown across the room, shattering, while a little girl sat in the corner, plugging her ears and humming. A cat stretching and curling on a deep shag rug. A whisper breathed closely through a kiss. A haggard man in an ill-fitting suit sitting slumped in a chair, staring at his old shoes. A large family gathered around a candlelit table laden with food, toasting and cheering. The curves of two naked bodies arching toward each other on black velvet sheets. A baby suckling from under its mother's uplifted shirt, as she rocks and sings slowly. Each window a story, each story replete with its own depth and complexity, its pain and joy, and they just kept on rolling in, at several hundred miles an hour, thousands of them, millions, rolling in relentlessly. I turned away.

When faced with magnitudes, we balk. The population of a city, the number of atoms in a human body, the size of the universe, none of it makes any sense. Even if we manage to catch just the edge of the thought, the vast curve of the whole idea that swells up enormously from there is more than we can wrap our minds around. We close down and turn away.

•

When I was in my twenties, I lived in Vermont. In the winters I would ski at the drop of a hat. Cross-country, not downhill. There were all sorts of places to go. State parks, resorts, golf courses, you name it, but my strongest memory is of a day spent in the woods of an old farmer. You wouldn't know his place was open for skiing. He didn't advertise in the papers and he sure didn't go out and track his paths, or serve hot toddies with cinnamon sticks around a fire in his living room. He just hung a hand-scrawled sign out front by the road, "Cross country. All day. $5.50." I liked the bit about the extra fifty cents. How'd he figure that?

The day I went was stunning. Clear-blue skies beneath which the world lay white and waiting, untouched. I went up and knocked on the front door. Fifteen minutes of stamping around on the porch later and countless raps on the door that gradually rose in bravado, just when I had decided there was no one home and turned to go, he came to the door, barrel-chest plaid in red-check wool, face smudged with a five-day beard, the butt of a cigar in one hand and a can of beer in the other. He took my five dollars and fifty cents and pointed a stubby finger across the road. From where we were, I could see open pasture and forest beyond. The trees were sparse on the flatland, thicker where they swept up into the hills, and north from there, solid forest, clear across Vermont. He said nothing and shut the door. A real curmudgeon I thought. Later, I realized I might have been wrong. I saw then that maybe, just maybe, he knew what I would find out there. And, that if he were offering me that, why speak?

I unloaded my skis, jumped the barbed-wire fence by the road, geared up, and headed out, cutting slim tracks through the soft snow. There wasn't a sign of life for miles. Not a peep or a scurry, not even a pawprint. I crossed the pasture and slipped into the forest, leafless and still, gliding through a silence broken only by the swish and cut of my own legs and the huffing of my breath pushing white clouds into the air.

A few minutes into the run, I stopped to adjust the binding of one of my skis. After fidgeting with it for a bit, I straightened up, pulled on my gloves, and leaned to start again when something moved in front of me. I froze. Just ten yards off, right there in front of me, a small, sleek animal had popped out from the snow. Bigger than a mouse, smaller than a fox. A weasel? A ferret? Would I know the difference? Its back was to me. It looked left, then right, before disappearing back under the cover of snow. I straightened up again, slowly, and inhaled deeply, realizing I had stopped breathing. Whatever it was came out again. I froze again. It came popping up like a knock-down carnie game, lifting its head into the light. But this time, just as it rose, a shadow fell to meet it, a blur of brown, and it was gone. Just gone.

I skied over. There was a long gash in the snow, starting out of nowhere, going nowhere, continuing straight through the snow for a yard, deepening, then ending abruptly in a little dab of red. Whoosh. Crunch. I looked around. Nothing for miles. Is that how it happens? You come up for a breath of air and life grabs you. Lifts you away on a clawed wing leaving nothing but stillness and a memory engraved lightly on the soft skin of the earth. Is that how it happens?

I skied for a couple hours, working up a sweat, making a broad circle around to the place where the flatland rose into foothills, stopping there to rest. Leaning into my poles, trying to keep perfectly still, I looked out into the forest. Just looked. Keeping very still. I couldn't help but wonder what might disappear next. Was it my time?

Covered in deep snowdrifts, the ground was mute, its edges softened to the point of abstraction. The forest was a frenzy of crooked vertical lines and undulating horizontal shadows receding into the distance beyond perception. The sky flowed through them from above, coloring the shadows blue. The whole thing was utterly still, as if I had happened on a forest set in crystal. Or walked back to the dawn of time and come upon my own world sleeping, yet to be stirred.

Behind each dark trunk stood another, and another yet. Each cast a bent shadow across the curved banks of snow, layered one upon the next, repeating in increasing complexity off into the distance beyond perception. Having been shed of its summer garb, the forest had no end, nothing to contain it, and I looked deep into the pattern of its weave and found my thoughts flowing outward through the warp and weft, slipping through, unstoppable. Past the lands of the farm, past county borders, past Vermont into Canada, hurtling through the naked world, drawn through it, up across the wilds of northern Quebec and out fast to the Northwest Passage, rushing through a seamless landscape, tree to tree, shadow to shadow, bank to bank, on and on, never ending. And in my mind, everything was still, out and across and through it all, not an iota stirred, not a single twig. And I began to feel very, very small; a quiet breath in the middle of it all. No more than a memory engraved on the soft skin of the earth. Or a thought, yet to be.

The snow became water, immeasurably broad. Chill turned to warmth, white into deep blue. I am ten, standing on the gunwale of a sailboat looking out across a borderless sea, my skinny legs shivering despite the heat. Happy voices beckon from the water, but I can't move. "Jump!" say the smiling heads bobbing in the gentle waves. But I can't. It's too big, too dark. What's out there? So I teeter on the edge, the sail flopping loosely behind me in a lazy Mediterranean breeze. A far-off buoy rings as it lolls over passing waves.

"Jump! Jump!" the heads shout again. So I jump.

Feet first, down like a lead weight, head under water, thrust full into the unknown, awash with fear. Is this when it happens? Whoosh, crunch. I bob back to the surface and await the first clutch of a muscular tentacle, a cold sharp bite. Is this how it happens? But the fear is of more than being eaten, as if that's not enough. It's the size. Where is the bottom of this thing? Where are the sides? There're none, right? It just goes on, forever. And then some. A liquid cosmos, undivided, infinite, filled with teeth and crumbling pieces of old things and God-knows-what, broken ships, half-bit fish, and an unlucky sailor drifting downward out of light into darkness, eyes wide, permanently aghast. And my toes are poking down into it all.

I feel very, very small. Alone in the middle of it all. No more than a dab on the wet skin of the earth.

A jellyfish comes bobbing by. It and I. Infinitesimal, flecks of dust on the waters. Just floating. Just there. And suddenly, I know. Right then, right there, beaded onto the glistening surface that runs unbroken around our planet, embedded in the multitude, intensely aware of my own fragility, I know. Not the Big Know, the little one. Not the Universe, but the self. I know the size of my body, lit by the goose-bumped edge of my skin. I know it precisely. Hear my heartbeats surging in my own ears. Had I never heard my heart before? Feel the sun hot on my head and salt on my lips? Warm salt that tastes like blood. And I know, suddenly and without question, I am alive.

I look now into a cold forest without end, and flow out through it, lost in its magnitude, overwhelmed by the complexity, and know, here too, I am alive.

I kick off my skis and flop backward into a snowbank,

socketed into it. A slender stem buried beneath the snow pops out and snaps against my face, stinging as it cuts. It shivers there, just inches from my eyes. The bark is studded with little pointed buds, tinted red and ready for spring. Why don't you freeze in winter? You should be brittle, hard as rock, yet here you are, young and supple. Each bud is attached to the stem by a slim nodule that attenuates and envelopes the bud like a closed fan, gradually lengthening toward the tip. The design is flawless, each layer no more or less than what it should be. A leaf, waiting to be stirred. A thought, yet to be. Waiting for spring. You throw yourself on the magnitude, spread out to the point of disappearing, expecting to be consumed, and find a point, a single minuscule point to latch on to. A bud on a twig, a jellyfish bobbing by. Caught suddenly by that thing, you pause and find there as well, yourself, just waiting there. Alive.

All people, I imagine, have similar experiences. Perhaps not in the ocean or a forest, but certainly at some point, when we're young but not too young, we all encounter the concept of infinity, and balk. Perhaps it will be when lying in bed before going to sleep, staring wide-eyed at a dark ceiling, picking out flecks like stars. The ceiling becomes the night sky and you find yourself propelled out into it. Up off planet Earth, out past the moon, past the other planets one by one, Mars, Jupiter, Saturn, into the darkness of interstellar space, past galaxy after galaxy, on and on whipping at immense speed toward its most outer edge. You do this for a minute or two, probably not more, and finally reach the limit of your ability to imagine. You falter and the cosmos evaporates, replaced once more by an ordinary ceiling. There are magnitudes we simply aren't designed to deal with. The number of people in a city. The seemingly limitless size of the universe. We cast ourselves out on the world in hopes of understanding its boundaries, and though we may not find an end to those infinities, if we are lucky, we might just find ourselves.

the name of the willow

The myriad connections that underlie the tangible form of all things in the world

At a place where the stream makes a long wide arc and the forest that surrounds it opens onto a meadow of wild grasses, the willow grows, a solitary figure on the riverbank. The tree has an unusual curve to its trunk and a lopsided pageboy cleanliness to the way its slender branches droop toward the ground. People say it is a willow, but over the months and years that I have spent visiting the tree, I have come to realize that, in fact, its name is not Willow as I first thought. No, things are not that simple.

To begin with, there is that strange bend to its trunk. The tree grows at the top of the bank about hip high above the river. It grows outward from the soil toward the river then curves skyward. What happened to cause that shape is that over the decades, each time the floodwaters rose and the river chewed away at the bank below the tree, the footing of the willow would loosen a bit and it would lean out just a little toward the river. Then for the next few years it would grow straight up again, reaching for the sky. The next flood came and it leaned again then grew straight in the ensuing calm. This, repeated countless times, caused the base of the trunk to grow in a curve. No other willow tree I have seen anywhere has this particular shape, so I think to properly call things as they are, this tree should really be called Riverbankwillow. It is not Forestwillow, growing lanky and tall between other trees, or Windyplainwillow, with its entire form canted away from the direction the wind comes from, or even Citystreetwillow, its branches pollarded back to gnarly stubs each year. No, it is none of those. This tree is Riverbankwillow.

The next thing that stands out about this tree, this particular tree, is that strange pageboy haircut. One winter, when the snow was deep and soft, I happened to pass by while skiing cross country and found a herd of deer surrounding the tree in a half circle like supplicants before an altar. They were nibbling off the tender ends of the willow branches. Right up to the height to which their pliant necks would let them reach, the willow was gradually being extinguished. When they left, the tree had a nice new haircut, but only on the meadowside of the tree. The riverside still hung long and luxurious toward the icefringed water. It is a style and shape that I have never seen in any other willow anywhere and made me realize that the tree has yet another, more descriptive name. Riverbankhungrydeerwillow.

On a fine spring day when a haze of small flowers brightened the edges of the forest, I wandered along the riverbank, and, as I neared the place where the willow grows, from a distance I saw a fox kit bouncing and skittering below the tree. First one kit, then two, then a third. All rusty backs and white bellies, popping legs and quick tails, little black noses as if dabbed on to make them that much cuter. The mother appeared from the den she had dug underneath the willow and in a flash the kits were all over her. She nipped at them to drive them off and trotted away, disappearing into the bright green meadow grasses. When she returned, she had a rabbit in her jaws. At the mouth of the den, she proceeded to tear off pieces of furred meat and pass them to the kits. When they were done eating, the kits fought over the bones for fun, and what was left over after that, I imagine, just rotted over time and returned to the soil. The blood and bones of the rabbit, the scat and piss of the kits and their mother, the fur they scraped off each other as they wrestled their days away, all of that eventually decomposed and trickled down into the soil to be absorbed by the roots of the willow. And that, too, is part of the tree. Riverbankhungrydeerfoxskulkwillow.

On my many trips past the willow, I saw many things, but there was one I never could see, even though I knew it was there. It was not invisible, simply hidden underground. The trunk of the willow swells where it reaches the soil and sends its shallow roots out in all directions. They can be seen bucking along beneath the surface. From there, smaller roots dive down into the soil and from them fork off a myriad of even smaller roots, continuing to split and fork until the individual lines are no thicker than a hair. But that is not where the tree ends. That is only where it begins. There, where the roots have attenuated to the point at which they all but disappear, they merge with another life, a fungal net called mycelium. The mycelium spreads out, not just around the tree, but throughout the entire landscape in a living network. The fungus secretes enzymes into the soil, breaking down potential nutrients so they can be absorbed and, once absorbed, transmitted to all the plants touched by the network, including the willow. The link between woody plant and fungal network is so close and integral, it is like they are simply extensions of one another. Riverbankhungrydeerfoxskulkmyceliumwillow.

I tried to climb the willow one day, to get up high above the river and look down into it in hopes of spotting trout. The bark of the trunk felt dry and powdery, and when I looked closer, I saw many small holes where insects had bored under the bark. Probably snout beetles, I thought, a nemesis of the willow that is the cause of many a tree succumbing to heavy winds. Nothing to do about it, not out there in the forest in any case. I suppose the beetles have as much right to live as the willow, although from my selfish point of view, I'd prefer the willow any day. OK, I thought. Where are we now? Riverbankhungrydeerfoxskulk myceliumsnoutbeetleborerwillow.

Summer came one year with a vengeance. I spent the night camping near the tree and, in the morning, did some fishing in the river. When noon rolled around, and the sun got too hot to bear, I lay down in the shade of the willow for a midday nap. A breeze nuzzled the threadlike branches until they swayed delightfully. Sunlight trickled through, turning into glittering rainbow starflakes. It is the sun, of course, that is responsible for all this. The tree I mean, if not everything else. It is the energy from those streaming photons of sunlight that underlies the growth of the tree, giving the chlorophyll in the leaves the power to split water and air and rebuild them as cellulose. It is the sun that is the mother at whose breast all plants suckle, including this lonely willow, so how could we not mention her in the name? Riverbankhungrydeerfoxskulkmyceliumsnout beetleborersunshinewillow.

In some cultures around the world, an ancestor's name is included in the name of a descendant. It can be as simple as Fredrickson—the son of Fredrick—or as complex as the baptismal name given to Pablo Picasso—Pablo Diego José Francisco de Paula Juan Nepomuceno Crispín Cipriano de la Santísima Trinidad María de los Remedios Alarcón y Herrera Ruiz Picasso—which includes the names of various saints and relatives. Now, there's a name that tells you something about a person, that tells you where they come from, what they're about. Likewise, if you were to really want to call this willow by its proper name, a name that reflects where it comes from and all the many interconnections that have shaped it into what it is, for better or worse, all the things that have fed it and all those that are feeding on it, if you wanted to include all those in its name you would end up with something longer than

Riverbankhungrydeerfoxskulkmyceliumsnoutbeetleborersun shinewillow. Much longer. By the time you said it, the tree would have long since grown old and died.

The botanical name of this willow is *Salix babylonica*. That has meaning too. Salix is the genus that means willow and derives from the Proto-Indo-European root *salik*. *Babylon-ica*, the species name, was given to the tree by Carl Linnaeus, father of modern taxonomy, back in 1736. He chose *babylonica*, which obviously refers to Babylon, because he thought that it was willows that were mentioned in the Bible as growing along the rivers of Babylon (although those trees were most likely to have been poplars). The name *Salix babylonica* is not without meaning, no, but the purpose of the name is to show how it is separate and unique from other trees. A weeping willow is not a pussy willow, so we have the two species *Salix babylonica* and *Salix discolor*. A willow is not an oak, so we have the two genera Salix and Quercus.

The purpose of all the names we give things is to separate them out from the pack, distinguish them from other things. It is an important and necessary step in using language to make sense of the world, and yet as a result of naming the things of the world in that way, we come to see the world as a collection of separate entities. We understand the world through the lens of differences rather than one of connections. If, instead, the names we gave things were more like Riverbankhungrydeerfoxskulkmyceliumsnoutbeetleborersun shinewillow, names that show not how things are different but how they are inextricably connected, then our entire worldview would shift.

A name like that is unwieldy. Agreed. You could never make small talk if every person and every thing had a name like that, so I don't expect a great rush toward giving names that reference all interconnections. But if I may suggest, just try doing this once or twice as a mental exercise. It forces you to see the world in a new way. To understand that the object before you, whether it's a tree on a bank of a river or one of the people in your life, is not a separate thing, but an amalgamation. A confluence of streams, an aggregate of interactions. And you are part of that, too.

wild in the city

A tiny garden that brings a patch of the
wild forest into the city

The city I live in is Kyōto, Japan's ancient capital. It's just over 1,200 years old. Perhaps sixty generations of people have lived here. Just thirty sets of gran'folk back to the beginning. For some reason it seems as if there should have been more.

Kyōto did not develop organically the way many cities do, beginning as a hunter-gatherer's camp then turning into a village, a village to a town, a town to a city as the population grew. Neither did it develop because of a natural trade route, a harbor or a confluence of navigable rivers, or at the base of a particularly important mountain pass. And it didn't develop for reasons of industry, such as being close to a valuable source of natural resources: salt, metal ores, or anything like that. No, Kyōto was built from scratch on a landscape that had theretofore held nothing but meadows and copses of bamboo. It was a kit city, built from a complete set of plans imported from China, a scaled-down version of Chang'an, the capital of the Tang dynasty. The original name of Kyōto was Heian, also borrowed from the Chinese. Chang'an means Long Peace, and Hei'an, Harmonic Peace. Heian was envisioned in its entirety before any work commenced and was then imprinted onto the land within a year of groundbreaking. Presto magico.

According to plan, the overall shape of the city was a large rectangle, infilled by a regular pattern of north-south and east-west streets, some large, some narrow, forming a grid of rectangular properties that were assigned by the emperor to the citizens according to their position in society. The larger and better-situated properties were assigned to those closest to the emperor, while the smallest ones went to commoners. In the centuries following, the city expanded past its original, idealized core but, until quite recently, it was still surrounded by stretches of agricultural fields. The area I now live in, for instance, where the flat basin floor begins to rise into a range of low mountains that form the city's eastern border, was still end-to-end rice fields until just thirty years ago. Now it's end-to-end buildings. Presto magico.

My house is at the end of a dead-end street, an alley really, only partly accessible by car. When it was built seventy years ago, there was nothing but fields and pasture around it, but now the house sits in the shadow of developments. A five-story wall of bland apartment buildings hems in one side, while a thick concrete retaining wall and pre-fab houses frame the other. When my house was built, it stood as an anomaly in its environment, a small work of man amid fields and meadows. Of course the fields, too, were works of man but, even still, I imagine that the house stood out clearly from its surroundings, an architectural blip in an otherwise botanical landscape. A tiny dot of brown amid the green. Now the house is consumed within the new city and yet stands once more as an anomaly in its environment. Organic within the industrial, a tiny dot of brown amid the gray.

In the back of the house is a small garden, a very small garden, no more than five by ten feet. It, like my house, is surrounded and enclosed. The frame of the garden is my house on two sides, an old cinderblock storehouse on a third, and the corrugated-tin wall of the neighbor's house on the fourth. The design of the garden is sparse, to say the least. There is only one plant, that is to say only one that remains present throughout the year, a broad-leafed aucuba. The Japanese call it *aoki*, Green Tree, and so it is, leaves and stems alike. The leaves, in fact, are variegated, decorated with little yellow-green dots as if drops of rain had been marked indelibly on them.

There are two rocks in the garden, one I brought from my old house (I had grown attached to it, figuratively speaking) and the other I found in the front garden when we moved in. Two rocks. No more. And, there is an old tree stump. A rather large stump considering how small the garden is. Before the tree was cut down it must have towered over the house, its trunk an overwhelming presence outside the sliding door that opens onto the garden. I can't imagine there was anything like a garden at that time. There wouldn't have been enough light. The stump now balances with the two rocks, making a triad of forms and creating the basic structure of the garden. Japanese artists tend to use triangles, or groups of three, as the basis for their designs. Triads, they feel, lend stability as well as dynamism. And so it was that I began this garden with a group of three.

The stump is rotting away. Rotting things are not, in fact, appreciated in traditional Japanese gardens because they symbolize death and decay. Come to think of it, I'm not sure rotting things are appreciated in gardens anywhere. I had toyed with the idea of hacking it out but, in the end, left it as it was. Although it is decomposing, and so clearly a symbol of death, it is also a "nurse log," with moss and some very delicate ferns growing out of it, and as such, is also a symbol of life. This little nurse log is nothing so grand as the massive fallen trunks found in the rainforests of Washington State that seem to spawn entire new groves on their backs; but even still, as the stump dissolves away, returning to the soil from which it originally sprang, it offers itself as sustenance to other, smaller plants. It has come to symbolize for me neither life nor death, but the continuity of the two. Not a beginning or a closure, but a cyclical path without end.

On one side of the garden, the ground is covered with small rust-colored stones that a friend collected for me from the mountains. He is a gardener and one of the few who still knows how to collect material from the wild. The other side of the garden, rising in a slight swell, is a bed of deep-green moss.

Stone and moss, geology and botany, opposites playing off one another.

I said that there is only one plant in the garden, the evergreen *aoki*, and that is mostly true, but seasonally there are more. In the spring the heads of small ferns sprout from the moss. Handfuls of them. These ferns are different from the tiny ones that grow on the old stump. They are called *beni-shida*, which would translate as something like Russet Fern, so called because when the fiddleheads first unfold, the leaves are not green but a bronze-russet color that lasts until the leaf has hardened. The green color, which takes over from the russet, fills in from the spine of the fern outward, chasing the redness to the fringes until only the outline of each leaf is tinged red as if it were made of a thin metal sheet that had been flashed into color by an intense heat.

By the standards of traditional Japanese garden design, I should be more severe with these ferns. As they poke out from the moss I should thin them until, at most, only two or three remain. That scarcity would be in keeping with traditional aesthetics. But I have a weakness for the ferns. For the nautilus shape of the fiddlehead, unfurling itself as if demonstrating for anyone who might be interested the mathematics of spirals. For the bronze color that washes through the young leaf, metallic-botanic. For the finely dentated edges of the leaves, as complex and deep as fjords. And, for the tender way the new fronds tremble at even the slightest breeze. So although I should thin them out, I don't, and the garden fills with tight fiddleheads, then spirals like ornate miniature walking sticks, then layers upon layers of triangular fronds that consume the floor of the garden. Instead of sparse, the garden becomes wild, like a patch of forest floor dropped onto my corner of the city.

I peek into this garden filled to brimming with ferns—in the morning as I dress, as I pass it on my way down the hall to the bath, as I undress for bed at night—and it stills me. I look, and for a moment, for just a moment, I walk in ancient forests, and am free.

interfaces

Seeing the world, not as forms, but as the interfaces between those forms

It came in the night, September 16, back in 1972. Mythic-scale rains battered Japan, brought up from warm southern waters by the winds of typhoon number 20. In the mountains above where I live now, there had been a brook running quickly down one of the narrow valleys toward my neighborhood. The name was, and still is, Otowagawa, the River of the Sound of Wing-beats. I like to think that the burbling of the brook over the many stones in the riverbed created a hum like beating wings. At some point in the past, however, the government came in and reworked the brook, widening it, straightening it, building a series of step dams to slow the flow. What had been six feet wide became sixty feet wide. The idea was to make it safer by opening it up and controlling the flow. Or perhaps the idea was simply to spend money on a local project that didn't really need to be done, to purchase local support for the leading political party. Those two ideas had become one and the same in Japan by that point, and controlling rivers provided an endless source of pork-barrel projects throughout Japan.

Despite the intention of creating safety through control, the reworking of the Otowagawa had the reverse effect. Widened, straightened, opened up, the brook—now a broad river—was able to gather far more water than it would have been able to do before and, when typhoon 20 brought the great deluge on the night of the 16th, all that extra water, and untold quantities of mud, stones, branches, and shattered trees, came barreling down the mountain into the sleeping village below. The little rivulet that had run between the homes, with its stone walls and small bridges, was completely overwhelmed as the mudslide ripped its way down the mountain. Two hundred and seventy houses were destroyed.

The solution was obvious. All the houses along the little waterway were removed and the six-foot-wide brook was replaced by an enormous culvert. The walls and floor of the culvert were made of poured concrete, and step dams were built along the way. The possibility of another overflow was all but eliminated. The solution to widen the river and line it with concrete was the kind that would be made by the manager of a factory complex where efficiency of production and worker safety were paramount. From that perspective, it was the right solution. If rivers are thought of as being simply conduits used to bring rainwater safely and efficiently from mountains to the sea, then the work done throughout Japan to rework the rivers and line them with concrete has been a great success. If, however, one thinks about rivers not as drainage ditches but as living vessels akin to blood vessels in an animal or the vascular system of a plant, then the whole conversation changes. And, as with any living system, one of the most important aspects of a river resides at its edges. The interface where water meets earth.

It is the nature of nature to be dependent on interfaces, those surfaces where two bodies meet. The first and most primordial of these is the flat surface of a leaf. Our planet would be nothing more than a hot rock hurtling through space were it not for them. There, in those paper-thin layers, is where stacks of chlorophyll turn sunlight into sugar, changing electromagnetic energy into chemical energy and thereby creating the foundation for life on the planet.

Tidal basins are another of the essential interfaces. Have you ever lived at the edge of an estuary, or even spent a day there? You look out across the open water and see the land on the other side of the inlet, perhaps a small island or two. You gaze at the quiet, light-filled surface of the water and then turn back to the work at hand. You cook a meal, read a book, attend to whatever the business of your day is. At some point later on, as if coming up for air, you look out across the water again, only it is not the same broad unbroken sheet. Instead, the islands have expanded and now the water has separated into channels. You go back to what you were supposed to be doing, look up again at some point, and, wait a second, now there are only lonely pools here and there. Back to work for a bit and when you look again there is nothing but reeds and mud and flocks of yellowthroats, cormorants, and gulls drilling holes across it all. The darn thing just won't sit still. Back to work and it all flows in reverse, growing wetter and wetter at each glance, in and out, ceaselessly. Wetted and dried throughout the day, tidal basins are stunningly rich ecosystems. There are creatures from land that come there to hunt or escape being hunted, when there is enough dry land to let them in. There are creatures from the ocean that do the same when there is enough water. And there are many more creatures that exist only in that intertidal zone, adapted to both wet and dry. Those interfaces, called ecotones, where two ecosystems meet and overlap, are hugely busy places. The place where salt water meets fresh, or any water meets land, or forests of trees meet grassy meadows, any of these overlapping places grows furious with life, containing species from both neighboring ecosystems as well as some more that live only in the ecotone itself.

For us, and by us I mean humans, the fundamental interface that first comes to mind may be our skin, that outer layer that separates us and protects us from the world at large. But in fact the most important interfaces for us are those that are internal. The linings of our intestines and lungs. Even though those interfaces are hidden away inside of us, that is where we are ultimately docked into the world. The great body of atmosphere that envelops our planet flows into us and out of us through the delicately folded surfaces of our lungs, and the great body of the earth, in the form of water, plants, and animals, flows into us and out of us through the impossibly long tube of our digestive system. They say that the whole thing is as much as thirty feet long but that really depends on how you measure things, and to what degree of detail. They say the coastline of Japan is about twenty thousand miles long, and surely that includes dipping in and out of the major bays and inlets, but what if you drew the line more carefully, in greater detail, so that it included in that measurement all the smaller coves or, not just the coves, but all the minute indentations of the rocky coastline on all the nearly seven thousand islands in Japan. What length would that be? Our digestive system might be thirty feet long or it might be three hundred. It could cover the area of a football field, as is often claimed, or, measured in more detail, it might be a hundred of those fields. However you quantify it, it is along the surfaces of those organs, the lungs and the intestines, that we as individuals are inextricably linked to the world we live in.

The boundary between two bodies always has more activity, more energy, than the bodies themselves. Throw a chunk of sodium in water and, boom! But, it is not the body of water or the lump of sodium that is the cause of the explosion. It is that very thin molecular layer where they meet. This is true of chemical reactions, of physical interactions, of natural ecosystems, and of human society. Interfaces are where everything happens, and our survival depends on our ability to see the world not as a series of discrete bodies—people, plants, animals, minerals, and so on—but as a series of complexly folded and layered entities.

# of arcs and circles

*The destruction of a machiya as
a springboard for understanding
evanescence in Japan*

From where I sit, there is a clear view of the demolition going
on across the street. The street is narrow and I'm on the second floor. Ringside seat. A large, tracked machine sits on top of
a pile of debris in the middle of the site. It's an excavator, but
the digging bucket at the end of its huge, jointed arm has been
replaced by a movable claw. The operator uses the claw to tear
at the little wooden house he's destroying, chewing away at it in
noisy gulps, steadily, methodically, ripping the house to pieces.
He sits calmly on top of his work. I stare, mesmerized, watching
a world I once knew come apart.

The machine is bright yellow but the claw and the end of
the arm, which has had all the paint scraped off it, is dull gunmetal gray. The claw reaches out and yanks on a slim, clay-
plaster wall. It wavers just briefly, shuddering, then snaps,

loudly, and comes down with a crash, raising a sudden plume of dust and sending the waterman scurrying about in a dither. It's his job to constantly spray the work to keep down the dust. He's been standing there all day squirting like he was trying to put out some eternal fire that refuses to be extinguished. Now he's scrambling all around the piles of clay and shattered wooden beams, spraying into the air, cutting lines through the clouds of dust as if he could knock them down. The clouds billow outward lazily, unchanged.

I can't say I really knew the old couple who lived in the house. I met them only once, but I had heard of them often from my friend and felt I knew them better than our single meeting should allow. The husband taught flower arranging. He was rather tall for a Japanese man of his age, lanky, with long, long elegant fingers. His wife, who remained throughout his life his careful assistant, was petite but efficacious, quietly busy, everywhere at once, taking care of things. Together, at their home, they ran a small school where students would come on Tuesdays and Thursdays for instruction in ikebana, the art of flowers. My friend was one of his students and once, when I had come by to meet him after class, I had been invited inside. The front garden I had passed through that day, with its gate and overarching pine tree, the simple but elegant entry hall and its shelves of students' shoes neatly arranged with all the toes pointing forward, and the front room where the younger students practiced, all of that is gone now, crushed beneath the pile of clay rubble. The machine keeps up its work, picking away at layers of my memories.

The old teacher took ill some time back and died, rather all of a sudden. His wife stayed on in the house for half a year but having no income of her own, and no apparent support from her family, she was forced to sell the property to pay off the inheritance tax. She's not alone. Most old homes in Kyōto are sold off for the same reason. In any case, she sold off the property and used the money to pay the fees of an old-age home to which, one fine winter's day, she was taken by her granddaughter.

In the past, in country villages in Japan, there was a custom, called *ubasute*, of carrying elderly people off to the mountains to die if they became too feeble to care for themselves and were a burden on their family or village. As depicted in *Narayama Bushikō*, a 1983 film by Imamura Shōhei, before being taken off, an old woman would break her teeth with a rock. Committed to death, she would no longer eat. I doubt the custom was uniformly practiced, existing only in those villages where the people were, for one reason or another, living on the edge of subsistence.

On that winter day, my friend told me, the granddaughter came with her husband in their van. The husband stayed outside and smoked cigarettes. His young wife disappeared inside and came back an hour later with her grandmother and an armful of round, fluorescent light bulbs. The grandmother and the light bulbs — the only two things she saw fit to extract from the old house before it was destroyed. She took the bulbs home. Grannie went to the mountains.

The operator repositions his machine to get a better reach on the middle of the house. Black diesel smoke belches up from the exhaust as he revs his motor to move. The waterman reacts automatically and sprays the smoke, scattering droplets across the hood of the machine. The operator looks up, surprised, thinking it's rain, then back at his overzealous assistant, frowning. The hose lowers and the waterman returns to making lazy patterns across the piles of clay.

The debate in Japan about why the old wooden buildings of Kyōto are allowed to be destroyed so readily, while so many well-preserved cities or districts of cities still exist in Europe, often returns to a particular argument. The difference, the argument goes, is the one between ki-no-bunka, the culture of wood, and ishi-no-bunka, the culture of stone. Japan, it is claimed, represents the former, Europe the latter. Wood is a soft material, the argument goes. It breaks down readily. Societies that build with wood build impermanently, expect to recycle their architecture, and idealize transience. Stone is a hard material, so it lasts virtually forever. Societies that build with stone build for longevity, they expect their buildings to last, and they idealize perpetuity. The argument concludes by stating that since Europeans are people of Stone Culture, they build for permanence, their buildings last for centuries, and so they have well-preserved historic cities. The Japanese, on the other hand, are people of Wood Culture; they build temporary structures that cannot last, so the architecture of their historic cities is now giving way to something new. Shōganai. It's simply inevitable.

On the surface this seems plausible. If you drop a stone and a wooden plank on the ground and leave them, the stone will remain while the plank will begin to rot in a month and be reduced to soil within a few years. At least it would do so that quickly in humid Kyōto. Yet, in fact, whether a building lasts for a long time or not has less to do with what it is made of than it does with the attitudes of its caretakers. The major force that destroys buildings in modern societies is not fire, or floods, or typhoons, or earthquakes, or weathering from rain and sun, it's people. We take buildings down, purposefully, because we no longer want them. We rip them apart with custom-made machines. Yellow excavators with articulated claws. We destroy them in war, by burning and bombing them, sometimes intentionally, more often collaterally, but it's we who do it nonetheless. And, with the immense physical power we can harness, we can do this to buildings made of stone or steel as easily as those made of wood.

Care lovingly for architecture, however, and you will find that even those buildings made of wood can last for amazingly long periods. Nishioka Tsunekazu knows this from experience. He is the head carpenter working on restoration projects at Hōryūji temple. The main hall of Hōryūji was first built around the time of the founding of the temple in AD 607. After that, it burned and was rebuilt in its present form around 690. Although it has been repaired as needed every few decades, and more completely every five hundred years or so, Nishioka led a project to completely dismantle, repair, and reconstruct it in 1942, 1,250 years after it was built. The wood it was originally made of was taken from cypress trees that were two to three

thousand years old when they were felled. According to Nishioka, wood can last in architecture for at least as long as the life-
span of the tree it was taken from, so Hōryūji, he claims, has at
least another thousand years left in it!

When people no longer need things, or if they hate them,
they destroy them—wood and stone alike. And they do so with
the greatest of ease. If people love things, however, they care for
them and make them last, if not in perpetuity, then at least for
time scales that dwarf a single human life. This, too, is as true for
wood as it is for stone. The reason that historic districts remain
in Europe is because the people living in and around them still
desire them and care for them. The reason they are being devas-
tated in Kyōto, like the building across the street from me now,
is because their meaning and importance to this society have
been lost.

The demolition operator shears through another wall and
it comes crashing down, sending the waterman into another
panic of spraying. Only half of the building is left at this point.
The operator turns his attention to loading what he has already
pulled apart into the back of a small dump truck. Old door panels taken from the house—the opaque *fusuma* and translucent
shōji—have been propped along the sides of the truck to make
them higher. The operator digs the claw into the rubble and
yanks out a clump of shattered beams, shakes them to remove
the clay plaster, then places the shards in the back of the truck.
A young man with bleached hair and purple work clothes darts
around the bed of the truck, lining up the pieces. When they are

done, a quarter of the house will be tidily stacked in the back of his little dump truck and he will drive off to the incinerator in the south of the city. He'll pull up the long slope that leads to the facility, drive inside the huge voluminous building, back his truck up to the gaping fire hole, and dump a quarter of someone's life into the heat. And some of my memories. The flames will rise to meet them as if to draw the fodder in. Hungrily.

One of the great examples of wooden architecture in Japan is Ise Shrine, which is ritually disassembled and reconstructed every twenty years, in the same form but of new wood. Proponents of development here claim that this regenerative process is quintessentially Japanese and, by association, that the wholesale destruction of traditional architecture that has been going on since the end of World War II is, in and of itself, just an aspect of traditional Japanese culture. The cashing in of temporary architecture. The truth of the matter, though, is that of the hundred thousand or so shrines around Japan, Ise is the only one to invoke the ritual of regeneration through its buildings. There are other regenerative rituals at shrines. These usually involve the construction of an object, often of rice straw, that is used in a festival and then burned or allowed to degrade naturally over time. Except for Ise, and some other very, very rare exceptions, shrine buildings themselves are not destroyed and rebuilt.

The cyclical, ritual demolition of buildings has always been very rare, but, historically, the dismantling of wooden buildings for other reasons was common—especially those in urban areas. This is true of temples, the residences of lords and nobles,

as well as the shop/houses of the townsfolk known as *machiya*.
This disassembling is not a sacred act; the buildings are simply
being moved to new properties or donated to others as gifts. At
times the structures are redesigned or reshaped, split in two, put
back together, heightened, shortened, added to, made smaller,
you name it. They are dismantled for any number of reasons
but never, never, were they smashed and burned as garbage.
Never! Until recently, that is. If Nishioka were here to see the
machiya across the street being demolished he would shudder.
Not because this old house is a national treasure, like Hōryūji,
but because the way it's being demolished is such an utter waste.
Discarding old wooden buildings like trash is in no way, shape,
or form traditionally Japanese, and it is only the greedy or short
of vision who could possibly claim otherwise.

It's suddenly quiet. I look over and find the operator jumping down from his machine, batting dust from his pant legs. The
waterman continues to spray for a while, wetting things down
before he goes off to lunch with the others. The machine sits at
the top of its little hill, tilted rakishly to one side, arm propped
on the ground as if resting. Only the back of the house is left
now, the deepest part of my memory, sliced open and bared.
What's left looks like one of those strange cutaway illustrations
made to show children how the insides of things work.

In plain view I can see the stone-floored kitchen, with its
stone sink and wellhead. In the half-light, it looks like a student
is still there, washing out his vase, the water so cold it turns his
hands red. He bears the pain knowing the flowers last longer

that way. What's good for the flower is good for him. And there's the stone step that leads up from the kitchen to the sitting room and, inside, surely I see the curves of small backs bent diligently over their work, selecting and setting branches carefully in their pots. A line for Heaven, a line for Earth, a line for Man. And there's the *tokonoma*, the alcove where the old teacher always presented his work for the students to marvel at. I see him working there now, setting into an earthenware vase a single *natsu-tsubaki*, a summer camellia, the bud as yet unopened. Not a flower, only a suggestion of one to be. Hints and implications. Lean closer. They yearn to speak.

The teacher pulls back from adjusting the flower and calls to his students. They gather from the other rooms, from the kitchen and the hall where they wait their turn, and congregate in the back room on the veranda by the garden. I, too, lean over to look. Past the bent arm of the excavator, past the shattered walls of the sitting room now split open and laid bare, past the cluster of eager students, I see the old man point his long slim finger, white as chalk, at the garden that waits, still verdant, for his tending touch.

My friend is sitting in the group. He sees me standing across the street, waiting for him to finish and waves me over. The teacher is discoursing on his garden and the wildflowers that he grows there, pointing out the *baimo*, *azami*, and *shirai-tosō*, telling their stories as if the flowers were old friends with whom he had taken a long and profound journey. Friends with whom no pretenses were left. His ideas are drawn out in stories but the point is clear. These flowers last no more than a week in the garden. Less in the vase. Ikebana is the art of transience, an alchemist's trade conjuring the magic of loss.

He finishes his talk and the students go back to their vases, their cut branches and flowers. My friend and I are asked to help carry some boxes of heavy iron vases upstairs. We shuttle up and down the stairs a few times and then, on our last trip, are asked into the back room by the teacher, who had come upstairs with us to show us where to stack things. He sits in front of the second floor *tokonoma*, a smaller and more delicate space than the one below, arranging a sprig in a delicate bamboo basket. The leaves are dull green and deeply serrated, the flower an inconspicuous tower of tiny white dots. "It's called *futari-shizuka*," he says. The quiet couple. How perfect. He sets just one frond of the flower in the vase, then takes a small dipper of water and, in a single sharp stroke, splashes it across the basket. The water splatters across the clay wall of the *tokonoma*, soaking in, leaving a dotted spray pattern. The flower looks fresher with droplets of water on it, the wetness of the wall recalls the mists of the forests where *futari-shizuka* grows wild. "You know," he says "it only lasts a few minutes," nodding at the water on the wall. "Just a few. Beautiful things always end too soon." The only sound is that of water boiling gently over a charcoal fire. We all sit very still, looking at a moment soon to end.

The teacher's wife breezes in, kneels down on the *tatami*, and starts making tea. She pours hot water in the pot, adds some tea leaves and begins wiping the cups while she waits for it to brew. Always busy, always quiet. The teacher sits with his back to the *tokonoma*, looking at us look at the flower. His wife peers into the pot, swishes it slowly in a few quick circles, and pours out two small cups worth of delicate green tea. She places them on a lacquer tray and reaches out to hand it to me, smiling. I lean forward to take it but our hands never meet. A sudden shadow falls across her face and the huge gunmetal claw comes crashing down between us, shattering the floor, sucking the old man and his wife down in a flurry of dust.

I turn away.

The beauty of transient flowers. I get it. Of water sprayed on a clay wall, yes, of dew on *hagi* leaves, yes, of new green leaves on spring maples the color of which lasts but a day or two, of their brief crimson hues in autumn, yes, yes. I get all of those. But the pathetic waste of this *machiya*, no, I don't get that. Where's the beauty? Tell me. Where's the magic in this loss?

Another crash, another flurry from the waterman. He pushes his thumb into the hose and sends a fine spray into the air, sweeping it across the rubble as if blessing the site. The afternoon sun comes cutting into the mist and shatters into a rainbow, a coat of many colors flung loosely across the soft curve of the air. It stretches above machine and ground, connecting them in a glittering arc. I get on my bike to leave but the image comes home with me and, later that evening as I lie sleepless in the dark, it returns and snaps into focus.

The rainbow is an arc. The arc just a fragment. The fragment a section of a larger circle, the whole of which cannot be seen. Like the rainbow, transient flowers and dew are just arcs. Small fragments of larger cycles. Their beauty, their magic, doesn't come from their loss but from the deeper understanding that they will return. They must. They are but part of a circle. What we see as transience is only a piece snatched out of the big picture. An arc snipped from a circle.

When Ise Shrine is dismantled, the wood is not burnt. It is not thrown away. It is carefully distributed among the faithful to use in repairs of their own shrines. The structure is sacred even after demolition. When the old teacher was young, the extra cuttings left over after making a flower arrangement would have been carefully bundled and set out in a corner of the garden. The plants returned to the soil. The cycle completed. And that's why a *machiya* sent to the fires holds no beauty. It's been removed from the cycle. All loss, no magic.

•

A version of this essay was previously published in Kyoto Journal, issue 50, 2002.

solace for the tumbling mind

Watching the mind watch the world

On the far side of the lake is a small farming village. The folks there grow the best vegetables in the world. Plump eggplants, bright-red firm tomatoes, succulent corn, and a variety of squash the likes of which I've never seen before. But what's even better than the veggies themselves is the way they are sold. The farmers just heap all these wonders on tables in a large shed at the edge of the fields and leave them there for passersby to purchase. No one oversees things. There is a small box on the table for you to put money into. Visitors from the city drop their coins in and leave with bags full of vegetables and a nagging sense of shame, knowing they could never experience such a thing back where they come from. When did we lose this, they wonder? This confident belief in honesty and trust.

The village lies near the lake, at the bottom of a long, south-facing slope held snugly between two arms of the mountain that rises behind it. Uphill from the village, rice paddies and vegetable fields rise in terraces up to the point where the mountain becomes too steep to farm. From there, plantations of cedar extend further upward, and beyond the cedars is a wild forest.

About halfway up the slope, on the edge of the cleared land, where the fields meet the forest, is a small shrine. A *torii* gate hung with a sacred rope marks the entry. To get to the shrine, visitors pass through the gate and walk along a narrow path that leads to the forested slopes, and there, enfolded within the shadows of the trees, they find two wooden buildings. The first is a prayer hall that is used for ritual gatherings and festivals. Directly behind it is the shrine itself, a small structure with a hugely outsized roof, the whole thing set up on stilts at least chest-high off the ground. The spectacular thing about the shrine, however, is not these two small buildings but the grove of massive trees that surrounds them. The trees can be seen from quite a distance away, popping out of the forested landscape, five or six huge cedars, the oldest being perhaps seven or eight hundred years old and so large in its girth that it would take several people, arms spread wide, to wrap around the trunk.

The villagers take care of the shrine themselves. As parishioners, as a group, they are known as the *ujiko*, the clan children. The design and construction of the buildings, the maintenance of those buildings and the shrine grounds, the annual festivals that take place there, all these are handled by the local villagers as they have been since the village was first settled back in time immemorial. The shrine is truly a local entity. However, on the front of the prayer hall is a small handwritten sign covered in plastic and pinned in place with thumbtacks. It instructs visitors on the proper means of paying respects. Approach, clap once, bow at the waist to ninety degrees, rise, clap twice. Pray. These signs show up at shrines throughout Japan, put up not by the local *ujiko*, absolutely not, but stuck there by the Agency of Shrines, a national institution. The villagers, I would have thought, already knew how to pray.

They know how to build their homes without instruction from above. The way to farm. The way to sell their harvest. How to care for their ancient shrine and the forest that surrounds it. And, they know how to weave the spiritual feelings that connect them to the land into their daily lives.

Back at the roadside stand, I pick through the corn, while my wife takes a pile of eggplant and a squash. We leave our money and drive home, refreshed not only by the country air but by the simple act of being trusted. I felt as if this farmer's faith in me made it so. His trust made me trustworthy. It was a sublime feeling. Imagine that. You can make someone's day just by trusting them.

•

Here my mind tumbled first, sliding easily into that quiet euphoria in which all the world was good. Who could not be buoyed by thoughts of a life based on trust and sanctity and abidance to natural rhythms?

•

On the way to the village another day, traveling along a side road that I don't usually take, I found a small junkyard where farm equipment was left to rust and rot. Weeds grew up high around them, vines curled their way up exhaust pipes, an old bird nest could be seen underneath the seat of one tractor, wildflowers burst out from the engine case of another. The junk screams out in the landscape appearing only as an eyesore and a welt on failed theories of economic and technological improvement. These machines were intended to free people from their labor and increase production and profits for the farmer, but instead they broke down before they were paid for and were replaced by a new generation of machines that only got the farmer further into debt. In fact, the machines do allow farming to be done faster, but the leftover time is not spent in leisure or cultural pursuits. Nothing of the sort. The farmers just use that time to head off to jobs in local towns or cities to make enough money to pay for the machines.

The manufacturers of the machines do not leave a small box at the village for farmers to put their monthly payments in. Big business allows for no such faith.

Later that day, down by the lake, the sky was clear, dotted only with a few white clouds, the languor in the warm air contagious. I slipped on some snorkeling gear borrowed from a friend and jumped off the dock into the cool lake water. The sudden chill cried, Awake! through all the cells of my body.

With renewed energy I flippered my way around the shallows, just looking for what I would find. Sunlight angled down through the water, shimmering in wavy stripes along the mud and stones on the lakebed. Small fish darted away as I neared, never too far away, just enough to feel safe. There were clusters of fine red threads in bundles by the shore, the hair roots of a willow tree. Further on, a collection of waterlogged branches that looked, at first, like elk antlers. And then, glinting in a beam of light, a bunch of old cans, some with their lids still half peeled back. Ughh. Why here? Of all places, here in this mountain lake where the word "pristine" still has a semblance of meaning.

●

Second tumble, my mind tripping over the piles of rusting farm equipment and old cans causally chucked into the lake, and landing flat-faced on the unforgiving ground of reality. Having wallowed so pleasantly in delightful thoughts of my brethren souls, of their trust and age-old ways of living in harmony with the natural world, now my mind was snagged on the crusty edges of wastefulness and callous indifference to the world that we also embody.

●

I flippered over to the cans, thinking that I would be a good citizen and pick them up. Pop them in the recycling bin on my way back to the cabin. But as I neared, I could see the snout of a sleek brown fish poke out of one. It looked at me. I looked at it. It retreated. I stayed. And for the next ten minutes we played that game. I hovering on the surface, breathing noisily through the snorkel. It darting in and out of its steel home, frantic at the sight of a visitor.

OK. So, who am I to say garbage? An eyesore to me, yes, with my preconceptions, but to the fish, well, I guess she's tickled pink with her new stylish home. Can it be then, that any and all of the effluent of our grossly wasteful, disposal society will prove of use to some other part of the chain of life on this planet?

A little fish lives in a spent can. Entire communities of mollusks, algae, kelp, and barnacles, as well as countless schools of fish, make their homes in the hulks of sunken ships as if they were so many community housing projects that had been sent down there for that specific purpose. And what about Chernobyl and Fukushima? No critters will settle in there, will they? If you think that, say hello to the bacteria that are populating the shattered rubble around the molten cores, the microbes that will turn into exactly those radiation-loving species that will populate the Earth after we humans finally nuke ourselves out of existence once and for all. You think it won't happen? The nuclear holocaust that turns the planet into a desolate wasteland? Well, in truth, I don't either, but if it does, then the creatures that will survive in that brave new world saturated in radioactive material will be the ones that evolved in places like Chernobyl and Fukushima. The ones that don't mind the taste of fissile material at all. Just like the creatures that didn't mind the scent of that stunningly corrosive element called oxygen, which was the cause of the first great extinction three billion years ago. The progenitors of other creatures that still thrive today in the oxygen-rich environment of our planet. Creatures like you and me.

Archeologists are always picking through the garbage of past civilizations. Whether on the floor of a cave or at the bottom of a cliff above which ancient peoples made their homes, the trash piles there provide a rich source of information about what people ate and the kinds of tools they made, among many other things. In those pre-consumerist societies, before the idea of built-in obsolescence took hold, or conspicuous consumption, or the notion that participation in the mercantile system was actually a sign of patriotism, before any of that, people likely did not have a lot of excess stuff to throw away. But when it came time to get rid of something, they just chucked it. No tidy disposal bins or careful removal from the living area. No, just toss it. On the floor, out the window, over the cliff. No matter. The idea that it was "garbage," or that it would somehow mar the beauty of the pastoral landscape, that notion was many millennia away from taking hold.

The little brown fish pulls back inside its prefab home. It is happy enough with that particular bit of discarded trash. In truth, some of the waste we humans discard, like the pile of rusting farm equipment, is only a temporary aesthetic problem. The iron is simply changing back into iron oxide, the state it was originally in when it was dug out of the ground as iron ore.

●

And there the mind tumbles yet again, wobbling like a new-born colt just finding its legs. It seems to all be a matter of scale. You look at something and see it one way, but if you pull back through time and space to see a much larger picture, or dive in through time and space to find the minutiae at the core of things, then everything changes. Imagine looking at things from the next closest galaxy, Canis Major Dwarf, from which our entire Milky Way galaxy appears as no more than a pinprick of light in the night sky, and then try to find that pile of rusting farm equipment. Imagine looking at things from the point of view of one of the eighty-six billion neurons in your brain or a mitochondria in that neuron or an atom of oxygen in that mitochondria. Where is the can with the little brown fish then?

●

This tumbling is surely a natural result of the mind cautiously exploring the world, but more importantly, for me at least, it has come to be a kind of therapy, a self-administered solace that I use to keep all things in perspective.

subtleties

*Finding beauty in the paucity and
rarefaction of Japanese arts*

It is just an hour past sunrise. I sit on the back porch of the cabin watching the woods. Not just noticing that it is there, or idly musing, but really watching the woods. It is entirely still, a painted landscape. The trees are all there, standing in front of me in plain view, undeniably, yet far too still — as if the whole thing was only a life-sized model someone set up next to the cabin when I wasn't looking. Not a leaf budges. Not the ferns close by on the bank that slopes up beyond the porch, not the tops of the tallest trees where I always look for the first sign of wind to assess what the lake will be like that day. The whole thing as still as a cat poised to pounce.

There is no motion but there are sounds. The chirp of an early-rising insect. A quick pattering across the roof above me. It stops inexplicably before the edge. A chestnut tumbling down? I watch the spot on the eaves where I heard it stop, waiting for it to continue and fall. Then a green blur leaps off and into the leaves of a nearby bush. A lizard.

And there are colors. And, oh! what colors. Greens and browns to feast the eyes. There are no brilliant greens, no turquoise or lapis lazuli, and none of the dark mineral earth tones like sepia or umber. No, the greens are those of leaves, the colors of chlorophyll. The browns are those of bark, the slightly reddish brown of cedar, and the gray-browns of oak, wild cherry, and beech. And behind it all, the pale light of a clear blue sky.

I sit and look, keeping as quiet as the woods themselves, moving my head only slowly to peer left and right, and try to number the colors. I can't. It is no more than greens and browns and yet, what a treasure chest it is, as if a symphony was to be heard in the harmonic resonance between just two notes. The spectrum of the greens begins with the dark green cedar leaves and extends through the pale colors of fern fronds and oak leaves, up to the bright yellow-greens of young maple leaves, translucent against the sky. Within each tree, even though the leaves are surely all the same color, the way the light and shadow falls through them allows for a hundred shades of the same green. And the tree bark, too, is not one color or tone, but a thousand subtly different shades, stippled and etched onto these woods.

The sun rises further and sends a slender beam of light skidding down through the trees toward the porch. It strikes near a glass of water that was left on the railing of the porch after last night's dinner. The sun rises and, at the same rate, the light creeps its way over to the glass. When that beam of sunlight finally eases itself into the water, it explodes, sending rainbows onto the wall nearby. They glow and expand, stretching and becoming paler as they lengthen. The sun shifts, the light beam gets hung up on leaves high in the trees, and the rainbow slowly evaporates.

The roof, walls, and floor of the porch frame the view of the woods. What I can see is laid out horizontally like a scroll painting. Motionless. Filled with light. Scanning across that scene, noting every leaf as best I can, I can see no two the same. Many close, none identical, and it is in that subtle complexity that the voice of the woods speaks. Not the brash tenor of the rainbow with its vibrant full spectrum of light, the woods speak in a whisper, a murmur, intimate and close, a voice that asks the listener to hunker down, bend in closer, and listen hard. To open the apertures of their senses as wide as they can be. To open and to seek.

In my house in Kyōto, as in most traditional houses in Japan, there is one room that has a display alcove, called a tokonoma. Toko means floor and ma means space. The tokonoma is a small, floored space, an alcove set apart from the rest of a room specifically for the presentation of artwork. One does not enter into the tokonoma, other than to clean it. The artwork placed within it is usually a long vertical scroll that is hung on the back wall, either a painting or a work of calligraphy. In addition to the scroll, at times a flower arrangement in a vase is set on the floor, or in some cases hung from a small nail in the wooden post that borders the space. Traditionally, the flower arrangement contains no more than three different plants, one each to symbolize heaven, earth, and man. There are times, however, such as during a tea ceremony, when the arrangement contains just one flower, known as an *ichirin*. To the side of the *tokonoma* is a second space that has a narrow shelf or two in it. There, a treasured ceramic bowl or bronze artifact may be displayed. Rarely are all these displayed together. Sparseness rules.

I recall visiting the former home of Dr. Albert Barnes outside of Philadelphia, which had long since been turned into a museum. The owner had been very wealthy and was widely known as a great collector of art. At his insistence, the house had been preserved just as it was when he owned it, so visitors could get a sense of how Barnes lived with his possessions. The striking thing about the rooms, which does not go long unnoticed to even a first-time visitor, is that the ceilings are very high and every square inch of every wall in every room is covered with paintings. His reason for displaying things that way, apparently, was not simply conspicuous consumption or the painterly equivalent of trophy rooms, but to compose the works in arrangements that had meaning to him. The shapes and colors used in one work were placed so as to riff off similar artistic aspects in another. Whatever his reason, the means of display sits in stark contrast to the method applied by tea masters of sixteenth-century Japan who birthed the original "less is more." Their approach was rarefaction. The elimination of any and all extraneous elements.

No unneeded space or ornamentation was allowed in the architecture of the tea houses. The result was that the classical dimensions for a tea-gathering room was just four and a half *tatami* mats or about eighty-eight square feet. There are even other tea rooms only half that size. The most famous of these is the two-and-a-halfmat tea house called Jo'an that was built for Oda Urakusai in the early seventeenth century. Jo'an is just forty-five square feet. There is one *tatami* mat for the host to sit on while preparing tea and one for the guest who will receive tea. For obvious reasons no more than one guest is invited at a time.

The diminutive size is an attempt to reduce the architecture to the absolute minimum size required for two people to meet within the confines of a room, to allow for the communion of two souls over a warm bowl of whisked green tea. In addition to the two *tatami* mats for host and guest, there is also a tiny *tokonoma*. This is essential. In the narrow confines of the alcove will be displayed a scroll that makes reference to the theme of the gathering and an austere flower arrangement that indicates the season, or rather the season-about-to-be because the flower is always a marker of what is soon to come. For instance, rather than a camellia blossom in full bloom, a camellia flower bud is placed in the vase, perhaps one that is just beginning to open and show a sliver of the white or pink petals within.

The gathering for tea, whether for one guest or more, is of course a meeting of humans for human purposes, ideally for the appreciation of art. It takes place in a space and time that is contextual, that is related, in the specific sense, to those few members participating in the gathering and, in the general sense, to the cadence of the seasons. This reference to the seasons takes the interactions within the room—highly personal but also, ultimately, inconsequential—and elevates them to a higher plane where they are given substance and inertia by those larger movements. The little meeting over tea is seen within the context of the revolutions of the earth, the cycles of life and death, the whole thing caught in spokes of the Great Wheel Turning and carried forward by that, moment to moment.

Not only was the space of the tea house reduced to its most fundamental dimensions, but so were the things put inside that space. No utensils, furniture, or other accouterments were allowed unless they were absolutely necessary. The result was a reduction to the absolute core elements. A fire pit to hold charcoal, an iron pot to boil water, a jar of powdered tea with a slim bamboo scoop to extract it, a ceramic urn filled with pure water, and earthenware bowls from which to drink the tea. That's about it. The entire gathering, in fact the entire culture of tea gatherings, thus became known as *chanoyu*—hot water for tea. That's all it came down to. The boiling of water. The sharing of tea.

Having rarefied the architecture and the things contained within it, the tea masters turned their paring knives on the only thing left—the human element. To begin with, clothes worn during a tea gathering are restrained in their color and design. Jewelry and other decorative symbols of wealth are not allowed. And it doesn't stop there. No unneeded movements are permitted either, the passage of the human body through space reduced to its most efficient, and thus graceful, form.

The net result of the process of whittling away at the space and utensils, and behavior of those participating in the gathering, was not lackluster drabness or tedium. On the contrary. In that most rarefied of spaces, the perceptive abilities of the mind and senses become amplified.

When a person is faced with an onslaught of sensory information, the mind and senses close down protectively, allowing that information in only selectively to prevent sensory overload. In the rarefied space of the tea house the opposite is encouraged. Because of the quiet, the intimate space, the limited palette of materials and colors, the mind and senses open up into a searching mode. Whatever one encounters at that time is seen, felt, and understood at a level of intensity normally not experienced. The austere environment of the tea gathering is purposefully designed as a tool to awaken the senses, to make them aware of minutiae and subtleties.

The pale light that enters through paper doors, too feeble to penetrate the deepest shadows of the room.

The taste of the tea, like liquid green sunlight.

The form of a flower, just one, plucked from the many so that it can be seen—really seen—as if for the first time.

The sound of water boiling, a quiet hiss like a stream flowing through pebbles or wind in the needles of a pine forest.

The scent of the reed mats like an autumn meadow.

The soft clay walls absorbing any suggestion of echo.

The weight and warmth of a bowl of tea, fitted snugly into the palm, smooth against the lower lip.

The dark polish on the end of the bamboo tea scoop where generations of hosts have touched it, ever so softly.

The woods around the cabin remains still. I look and look, no longer seeing the greens and browns but absorbing them. They seep inside me as dyes into raw fibers. Though my skin will not change hue, I feel myself growing forest-colored. And then a leaf moves.

Just one, high in a tree, seen far in the distance through many trunks and gaps in the leaves. It must be broken at the stem because it moves wildly, fluttering round and round itself. Then another moves. And a third, and with that, the forest comes to life.

Over the course of the next two hours, the movement in the air grows steadily from nonexistent to gentle breeze. Insects join in a chorus, one by one, cicadas providing the greatest volume. A dragonfly longer than my hand, black with bands of gold spaced evenly along its pencil body, comes clattering into view, hovers, peers into the porch, then clatters away again. Bees of all shapes and sizes show up, probing around the sticks and bundled reed curtains stored in a loft beneath the ceiling. A dark moth flutters about the floor of the porch like a torn shadow nudged along by the breeze. The *uguisu*, my favorite bold-voiced warbler, adds its song, high and sweet, from deeper in the forest.

I have been here three hours and I'm not bored a bit. I will sit here many more hours this summer, perhaps over a lifetime, and the acute palette of greens and browns, dappled with light into a million shades, will never grow tedious. And when I leave this place, I will take the subtleties of the woods in my heart and carry them with me through my days. When I work, when I walk, when I meet with friends, when I garden, I will do so with the woods in my heart.

a garden by any other name

*Understanding the meaning of gardens
through the words used to name them*

Winter has come and gone. Spring arrived last week in full regalia. Warm breezes, flowers popping, the scent of rain-wet soil, birds shredding the air with their irrepressible songs. The mind turns to picnics in fields of daffodils but, given the paucity of those in the immediate vicinity of Kyōto, the body heads for a temple garden instead. Sitting on the veranda, wide enough and sheltered enough to be considered some species of outdoor room, I have a wonderful view of the garden. A pond. A pine. An old earthen wall beyond which lies the next temple over. What is this thing really, with the pond and the pine? What's at the heart of it? And why do we call it a garden?

What's in a word? A rose by any other name ... well, you know the old saw. But perhaps the Bard got it wrong with the idea that a sweet scent is the essence of a rose. The etymological root of the English word rose is *rós*, which in a Proto-Hungarian language means thorny or scratchy. In Japanese, the word for rose is *bara* and that derives from *ibara*, which means—does it need to be said?—thorny or scratchy. So, perhaps we should really be saying a rose by any other name would cut as deep.

The rose/*bara* example notwithstanding, the words used to describe things in different languages often reveal differences in the custom, culture, and mentality of the peoples who came up with the names, and so it is with the English word "garden," and the Japanese word *teien*, which refer to the same thing but have very different origin stories.

The English word "garden," etymologically, derives from the Proto-Germanic *gardan*, and before that from the Proto-Indo-European root *gher*, which means to grasp or enclose. It would seem that the ancient peoples living on the lands between India and England, in order to protect themselves from the outside world, built a structure around their dwellings. Whether this was a stone wall or a wattle fence or some combination of those, this defensive barricade was called a *gardan* (Proto-Germanic) or *garda* (Old Frisian), *gardo* (Old Saxon), *garto* (Old High German), and *geard* (Old English). I'd like to think it was wild boars and bears that these folks were defending themselves against but it seems that what they were afraid of was more likely to have just been other people. So, the ancient *gardan* was a protective barrier built around a dwelling to create a safe space within.

In a later time, as human culture began to develop into more complex forms, people gathered all manner of natural materials within that protective boundary and created places of comfort and beauty inside those safe zones. There may have been water to parch one's thirst, or shade under arbors in which to find shelter from the beating summer sun. Trees and shrubs and grasses with fruits and flowers offered pleasing tastes and colors and scents. In time, these places of respite and beauty that had been developed within the enclosing boundary, within the *gardan*, took the name of the enclosure and came to be called gardens themselves. If the Western garden is understood in this light it is fundamentally a place apart from the terrors of the outer world, a place that has certain essential qualities drawn from the surrounding natural world but is inherently separate from it.

Compare that to the Japanese *teien*. The word *teien* is composed of two parts: *tei* and *en*. Without going too deeply into the arcane complexities of the Japanese language, suffice it to say that in ancient times, before Chinese culture, including the kanji writing system, was imported to Japan, the words *tei* and *en* were pronounced *niwa* and *sono*, respectively.

Niwa was used to refer to an area, a certain precinct as it were, that people used in their daily lives. It could be the area of the sea to which they took their boats to fish or to dive for mollusks, urchins, and kelp. It was used this way by Kakinomoto no Hitomaro in a poem he wrote that was included in the great compendium of ancient poems called the *Man'yōshū*. As another example, *niwa* could refer to that section of a forest or meadows that was used by a village for hunting, as in the expression *kariniwa*. Or, as in the words *kamuniwa*, *saniwa*, and *yuniwa*, the word *niwa* can refer to a place in nature that has been purified for the purpose of religious ceremonies. The important thing, the thing that links all these words, is that in the beginning, long before the culture of gardens developed in Japan, the word *niwa* was used to describe a place within the natural world where people went to carry out some activity, whether it was gathering food or praying to their deities. People entered and used the *niwa*, but they did not change it or reshape it in any way.

Compare this to the word *sono*. *Sono* refers to a very different kind of relationship between humans and nature. The *sono* brings to mind an agricultural landscape, that comforting atmosphere of a pastoral place that speaks of human care and bounty. Whether it is the terraces that are carved into a slope to form rice paddies, or the land that is plowed and cleaned and fertilized for crops, or a plot filled with medicinal herbs, or the neat rows of orchard trees, the *sono* is a built place. A section of the natural world that has been manipulated and reshaped for the benefit of people.

Niwa is section of the natural world, untouched, that people enter lightly to use, and *sono* is one that has been entirely recomposed to fit the needs of the people using it. These paired aspects of wildness and control lie at the heart of the Japanese garden. In the garden, *niwa* and *sono* are skillfully merged into one entity and one word, *teien*.

Look there at the old pine tree, the twisted branches of which leap out over the pond. They appear for all the world as if they had been blown into that shape by unforgiving winds over the course of centuries, and yet the tree is only sixty years old and the shape it holds was sculpted into that form by the skilled hands of three generations of gardeners. A human-created evocation of wildness. And the stones along the edge of the pond that hold it in place against erosion. Each one is different from the next, set higher/lower, protruding/receding, so that the whole appears to be irregular cliff-faces along the seashore rather than a purposefully built garden element. Each of these is a depiction of the wild, expressed through the controlling hand of the gardener.

And, not just in the details of the garden. The overall design incorporates this merging of wildness and control, too. In the foreground, just beneath where I sit on the *engawa*, is the *ama-ochi*, a gravel dripline intended to catch rainwater falling from the roof. The sides of the trench are held in place with old roof tiles set on end, which form two parallel lines, straight yet rippling. Beyond that clearly manmade element is a patch of mossy ground and then the pond with the old pine tree hanging over it. At the water's edge, *yamabuki* shrubs droop their pendulous stems over the water, the yellow cascade of flowers sent skittering over the surface of the pond. Behind the *yamabuki* is an earthen wall, its plastered clay surface providing a carefully controlled background, a mute scrim on which to read the irregularity of the garden. On the other side of the wall is a *mokkoku* tree, billowing up above it like a green cumulus cloud. Beyond the tree, is the broad tiled roof of a temple sweeping up to a crisp ridgeline that sits proud and sharp against the afternoon sky. The dripline, pond, flowers, wall, tree, roof, sky are all alternating layers of elements that speak of wildness and control, all woven into one scene.

When we come to a garden, it is not to lose oneself in the garden, it is to find oneself there. To feel that inner being that longs to be wild again, to run through the ancient *niwa* that existed long before the world was so thoroughly domesticated. And, at the same time, to feel that inner being that longs for control, to lay a careful hand on the world and shape it into a place of safety and beauty. To feel the inner need for both wildness and control, in the same place at the very same moment. That is why we come to the garden.

karesansui

*Thoughts on creating contemporary dry
landscape gardens—what are often
called Zen gardens*

You can watch a summer storm descend upon you from across
a valley. Black clouds boil above the distant mountains and you
find yourself just standing there, watching them approach, the
air pressure dropping in a frightening headlong dive. Lighting
strikes somewhere across the valley, then moments later, only a
hundred yards away. The sky splits open and releases a deluge
of hail upon the world, tearing through leaves and pitting the
paintwork of hapless cars.

    With earthquakes, there is no warning. No theatrical
approach. The assault is instantaneous.

    Living in Japan means living with earthquakes. They may
come at any time, barging into your living room or place of
work without a hint of forewarning. Most often, they appear
as only a tremor, a quick rattle or thump. The walls shake, some

dust falls from the ceiling. A pendant light in the middle of the room sways. You stand, stock still, heart in your throat, eyes wide, ears cocked to listen for what comes next. Is this the big one? A moment later, realizing you have stopped breathing, you take a slow breath and grin or chuckle as if it were all nothing. But it is not all nothing. And it will come again. On that you can depend. The world is in motion and it cannot always move without breaking things.

Japan has the dubious fortune of being located at the convergence of not two, but four tectonic plates. Two of them, the Pacific and Philippine Sea plates, lie to the east of Japan under the ocean. Moving slowly westward, around two or three inches per year, those plates slide down underneath the Okhotsk and Eurasian plates on which the islands of Japan sit. The resulting friction and uplift is what causes Japan to be. The mountains rising from the sea that form Japan, and its one hundred active volcanoes, are all a natural result of the forces that lie hidden beneath the ground. As the plates grind and tear at each other, they understandably jitter and rattle from time to time, about 100,000 times a year, of which about 1,500 can be felt. On average, in a given year, one of those 1,500 will be devastating. But that is only the average over a century. In reality major quakes don't come in orderly fashion, once a year. They come unexpectedly, in clusters that even to this day are beyond prediction.

Earthquakes are called natural disasters but in fact they are not so destructive for life forms other than humans. Birds and winged insects lift into the air for a time at the first rattle and hover until it is over. Rabbits and deer run themselves in panicked circles, then go back to grazing a minute after it is all over. Plants are not bothered by the shaking, and if they end up shoved an inch or a yard from where they started, it doesn't matter. The sun shines just as well in that new spot as where they were before.

No, it is we humans, with all our built structures, who suffer. Buildings topple, automobiles skid off highways, dams and levees burst. In fact, when you step back and take a look at the effects of tectonic plate movement on a planetary scale, the negative effects of earthquakes and ensuing tsunami notwithstanding, the results are almost entirely positive. Creative, not destructive. The very landscape of Japan has been born of it, from volcanoes like Mount Fuji, which is the symbol of Japan, to the ordinary granitic hills that cover seventy percent of its landmass. Tectonic plate movement is the mother of Japan.

•

Japan's *karesansui* gardens are often referred to as Zen gardens in the Western press, although that expression is not Japanese in origin and these gardens are only tangentially related to Zen Buddhism. The word *karesansui* is written with three characters. *Kare* 枯, which means withered or dry, *san* 山, which means mountain, and *sui* 水, which means water. *Kare* refers to the fact that the gardens are made without the use of water, no brooks or ponds, and *sansui* is the ancient way of saying nature. The mountain is the quintessential *yang* element of nature: upright, solid, everlasting. Water is the quintessential yin element of nature: horizontal, fluid, everchanging. Mentioning the two archetypical elements of nature together, mountain-water, was a simple way to refer to all of nature.

The *karesansui* gardens are abstract expressions of nature, but the understanding of what nature is and how it works, which underlies those gardens, is that which existed in Japan before the introduction of systems of scientific thought in the eighteenth century. This traditional understanding of nature was, at that time, informed by the concepts of Buddhist, Taoist, and Shintō religions.

As an example, from Buddhism came the concept of Mount Sumeru, which the Japanese call Shumisen, the central mountain of Buddhist and Hindu cosmology. The image of this mountain as the axis mundi of the universe was one that was expressed abstractly in traditional *karesansui* gardens. From Taoism came the concept of *yin* and *yang*, the harmonically balanced dual aspects of nature. The classical form of a *karesansui* garden—a number of stones representing mountains, set in a field of raked white sand that represents water—is an expression of this duality. From Shintō, the native religion of Japan, came an understanding of stones as being not simply chunks of mineral but as points of connection to the world of the *kami*, the god-spirits that inhabit nature. The *iwakura* prayer stones, which predate gardens by millennia, are an example of this.

When the people of Japan during those medieval and early

modern times looked at the landscape, which given the landscape of Japan meant they were looking at mountains, they understood those mountains in a way that was informed by the teachings of Buddhism, Taoism, and Shintō. They did not see them as the result of the movements of four massive tectonic plates that underlay the very land they stood on, as the bedrock being bucked up from below. If they had seen the mountains in that light, not only as the realm of the *kami* or the earthly expressions of the sacred Shumisen, but also as the visible result of an enormous force that lay hidden in the ground below them, what *karesansui* garden would they have created then?

That is the question that led me to create just such a contemporary *karesansui* garden in the outdoor courtyard of a new building in New York City. The garden is called Thrust! (including the exclamation point for the proper effect). The materials and design are drawn from traditional *karesansui* gardens. Stones and moss are the only materials, and the overall design includes a great deal of what is called *ma*, or empty space, as do traditional *karesansui* gardens. The underlying theme of the Thrust! Garden, however, is the vast unseen power of tectonic plates, the movement of which is concealed until one realizes that the very mountains themselves are the revelation of that hidden power. In the Thrust! Garden there is a single upright stone, being seemingly propelled out of a field of smaller stones and moss that look like they, too, are being drawn upward by the force. The hidden being revealed.

In another place, also in Manhattan but this time on a

rooftop, I made a *karesansui* called the Still Point Garden. This time I was interested in the concept of singularity. Singularity is a word that has as many meanings as there are people who use it. To the mathematician it means one thing, and to the cosmologist or the theoretical physicist something else. The Penrose–Hawking singularity refers to how gravitation can produce black holes, while another kind of singularity refers to the infinite density that caused the Big Bang. The Still Point Garden features a single upright stone in an expanse of flat river stones laid in a fishscale pattern. The standing stone creates the image of a still point within a field of chaotic energy.

The Jesuit priest Pierre Teilhard de Chardin proposed a singularity he called the Omega Point, a confluence at which life on earth attains a final point of unification. According to his proposal, living entities on earth create first a biosphere that envelops the planet. Next, Homo *sapiens*, the wise-man or thinking-man, develop a noosphere, a layer of cognitive existence, which, in its final stage at the Omega Point, becomes separated from the physical world to create an overarching metaphysical entity. I expressed this concept in a temporary *karesansui* garden built at Daigoji temple as part of the Kyōto Arts Festival. In an open courtyard that surrounds the temple's thousand-year-old pagoda, I created a field of white sand that rose up into a mound in the shape of the Greek letter omega, Ω. The omega and the pagoda together formed a symbol expressing the similarities between Chardin's concept of release from the physical based on Christian and technological thought, and the Buddhist concept of nirvana or the liberation from the cycle of birth, death, and rebirth.

The first *karesansui* garden I built that used a contemporary understanding of nature as the basis for its design was the Spiral Garden. The setting was a thatch-roofed house in the mountains outside Kyōto, which happened to be the oldest extant residence in Kyōto City, built almost four hundred years ago. The house is L-shaped, the two wings and a separate storehouse enclosing a courtyard in which grew a maple tree that had a subtle spiral growth to its trunk. I extended that spiral out and across the courtyard in a sweeping pattern of moss and white sand. The spiral shape is certainly not the only basic structure in nature, but it is a fascinating one that appears in forms as small as the microscopic double helix of DNA, up to the incomprehensibly large expanse of a galaxy, the arms of which spiral outward from a center dense with stars.

As I write this, as if on cue, there is a slight tremor, one of those gentle shimmies that lies on the cusp of awareness, one that we feel and disregard in almost the same moment. And, yet, I can't help but accept it as a subtle reminder from the Great Beneath. One that says, yes, I am still here. You will not forget me.

the bipolar twins of japanese art

Understanding the fundamental
Japanese aesthetics of shin and sō

Tsukiyama teizō den is the name of an illustrated gardening treatise published in 1735 by Kitamura Enkin. The title translates literally as *Teachings on the Making of Built Landscapes and Gardens*. Nearly a hundred years later, in 1828, Akizato Ritō published a follow-up treatise, *Tsukiyama teizō den kōhen* (kōhen means sequel). In this second volume, Akizato introduces the idea of a tri-part system of categorizing gardens into Formal, Semiformal, and Informal styles. The term he used for this, *shin gyō sō*, was borrowed from the culture of the tea ceremony, which uses that same tri-tier system to categorize everything from tea trays to flower arrangements. This reminds me of the way some Japanese restaurants rank meal selections as *shō chiku bai*, pine bamboo plum, in which pine is the most elaborate and expensive choice, and the other two follow, becoming simpler and less expensive. By the time Akizato published his sequel, *shin gyō sō* had become just like *shō chiku bai*, in the sense that it was a stereotypical way to arrange and package a complex culture in order to make it more accessible and, as always seems to happen in the long arc of cultural development, more marketable.

This was not always so. The culture of drinking tea as an art form is known by the hyper-understated moniker *chanoyu*, "hot water for tea." When *chanoyu* was first being breathed into life by creative types back at the end of the fifteenth century, in cities like Sakai and Kyōto, what they were interested in was just the twinned aspects of *shin* and *sō*. *Shin* is written with the character for truth 真 and *sō* with the character for grass 草, but don't let that confuse you. *Shin* and *sō* are not describing truth and grasses. They are labels for two aesthetics that would come to underly *chanoyu* culture and, later, to permeate all of Japanese culture. Here, just a quick digression about pronunciation. *Sō* is pronounced as you would imagine, like the word "so" of "so what." That one's easy. The pronunciation of *shin* is a combination of the English words "sheen" (the result of polishing) and "shin" (that part of the body between the foot and knee). It has the vowel sound of "sheen" but is pronounced quick and sharp like the word "shin." Give that a try.

Getting back to history, the early development of *chanoyu* begins with the importation of an already high-developed culture of tea drinking from China. The practice as it was imported was formal, and the accoutrements and utensils used, whether a brass flower vase, a porcelain tea bowl, or a lacquered display shelf, were finely finished goods. At the end of the fifteenth century, and through the sixteenth, the practice of tea in Japan was redesigned by a number of creative people. The Nanbōroku, a record of tea culture from the end of the seventeenth century, mentions a man named Murata Shukō (also, Jukō) who lived at the end of the fifteenth century. It describes his teahouse as having been built in the *shin* style and depicts it as a formal building, almost like a little chapel, with white-papered walls and a curved hip roof that was commonly used for small halls in Buddhist temples.

Whereas his own teahouse had been built in the formal *shin* style, Shukō was in fact an early proponent of incorporating into *chanoyu* new and different elements that were of Japanese origin, elements that were more natural, organic, serendipitous, and spontaneous. This was proposed by Shukō as a counterpoint to the formality of Chinese culture. In a letter to a provincial lord who was an avid practitioner of *chanoyu* himself, a short note that has become known as The Letter of the Heart, Shukō writes, "Critical above all else in this way is the dissolution of the boundary line between Japanese things and Chinese things." Under his influence, and that of other tea masters who followed during the sixteenth century, the practice of *chanoyu* began to shift away from that imported Chinese formality toward a uniquely Japanese mode of tea culture in which tea gatherings employed "imperfectly natural" utensils and were held in simpler, rustic teahouses known as *sōan*. And there we have it, from Shukō's *shin*-style teahouse to the later *sō*-style teahouses—the initial referencing of *shin* and *sō*.

•

What are these twinned yet polar aesthetics of *shin* and *sō* referring to? What is the driving force behind each of them? It's
elegantly simply really and, at the same time, completely fundamental to Japanese culture as it would develop through the
Edo period and beyond. *Shin* is the aesthetic of human control,
while *sō* is the aesthetic of natural complexity. When a person
in the process of creation has an exact idea of what they want
to make—precisely what the size, shape, color, texture, finish,
and so on shall be—and bring all their physical and sensory
skills to bear to accomplish that, the object created is in the
shin mode. When making a woven tray, for instance, they will
decide that the bamboo will be split to a width of two *bu* (about
one-quarter inch) and sliced down until only the outer skin
remains, then woven in a precise double-layered, hexagonal
pattern known as *nijū mutsume*. They imagine this, will it to be
so, then make it so. That is the spirit of *shin*. Complete control.

When, however, a person in the process of creation under-
stands that they are offering only a partial guiding hand and
that the preexisting nature of the materials they are using and
the natural proclivities of the creative process also play a large
role in forming the object to be, that thing will end up in the *sō*
mode. If making a tea bowl, they will form the clay loosely into
a bowl shape by pinching it with their fingers, cast a glaze across
it almost haphazardly, then leave the rest up to the kiln gods,
stepping back from the process to allow those other entities to

bend and warp the work with their heat and coat it with a complex finish of melting ash. That is the spirit of sō.

Shin is about a person willing something to be as they had imagined it would be.
Sō is about sharing that creation with other elements of the natural world.

Shin is about acquiring complete control over the creative process.
Sō is about relinquishing that control.

Shin is about human mastery over the world.
Sō is about seeing humans as an integral but small part of that world.

If there are porcelain ceramics created in a wholly symmetrical way, with delicately brushed paintings on the glistening surface, the whole an ode to perfection, then there are also wood-fired ceramics made of gritty clay that crack and slump in the heat of the kiln and acquire a glaze from the natural process of burning wood that no human hand could ever replicate.

If lacquer can be applied in multiple layers, each one polished before receiving the next so that the completed black surface is akin to a dark mirror, then there is also a basket of woven bamboo covered with a gnarly dark lacquer that looks like nothing so much as the sediment of a hundred years of soot.

If temple halls are made from massive posts and beams of wood that have been cut and planed to precise dimensions and lifted up into a cathedral of axial symmetry, then there are teahouses made of slender natural timbers, some still with the bark on them as if just moments before they had been growing in the nearby forest, the whole laid out in an entirely situational manner.

If flowers and branches can be gathered into complex arrangements that follow age-old rules of balance and construction, so can a single bloom be gentled into a vase, artlessly capturing the essence of a season.

Of course, the world is not black and white. If there are objects that seem to be squarely expressing the essence of *shin* or *sō* exclusively, so too are there those that have some quality of each. Thus the appearance of the third member of the club, the *gyō* aesthetic that is a medium between its more rigorous siblings, or a combination of both of them.

But for me, the interesting thing here lies in the spiritual stance of *shin* and *sō*. As a designer, as a creator, which are you? Do you lean into the world hard, set your hand upon it and lay down the law of how things shall be? Or, do you enter into a kind of primordial dance with the world, nudging here and there, suggesting this or that, then sit back to watch what the world will make of what you began?

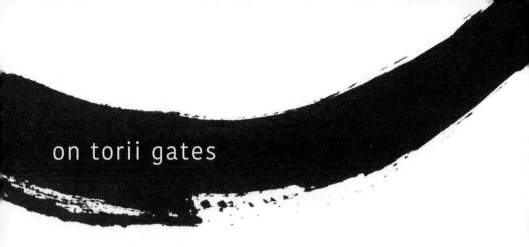

on torii gates

On the true meaning of the distinctive gate found at the entry to shrines: its name, shape, and color

It was a clear day in mid-October. I left the house early to beat the crowds and made my way south to Inari Shrine in Fushimi. Walking up from the local train station, the route passes through streets lined with shops catering to the many tourists and ends up at the grand flight of stone steps that ascends to the main hall. The hall is situated in the middle of an open court-yard with many smaller sub-buildings surrounding it. If you are coming to pray, the main hall is the prime destination.

The *kami* enshrined within is Inari Ōkami. Initially a deity of fertility, whether Inari is male, female, or androgynous, is not clear. Understandably, the deity of fertility soon became the god of bountiful harvests, in particular, the rice harvest, as is seen in the name, which translates as Great God of the Rice Cargo. In the medieval period, Japan's economy developed around a mercantile system that used rice as one of the main means of payment, perhaps more common than coinage for large payments, so Inari also became the tutelary god of prosperous business.

Even after the economy shifted away from rice to cash, and now on to electronic payments, Inari still remained the God of Business. Many businesses keep a small shrine to Inari inside, and some that own their own buildings have larger shrines to Inari installed on the roof. Business owners make small offerings to those mini-shrines each day and may visit one of the nearly three thousand Inari shrines throughout Japan at important junctures during the year. In addition, as a means to show respect to Inari and beseech blessing for one's business in a big way, businesses donate a *torii* gate to the main shrine in Fushimi. There are nearly one thousand of those now, lining the paths that lead from the main hall, up to the top of the small mountain that rises behind it.

It is these *torii* gates that are the most famous aspect of Fushimi Inari Shrine and perhaps, along with Mount Fuji and the Golden Pavilion, one of the most widely known images of Japan. The countless orange gates at Fushimi Inari, standing one after the other ad infinitum, forming a virtual tunnel that winds up the mountain, are something many people around the world can point to and say, "That's Japan," even if they know nothing else about it. In truth, the experience of walking through that endless corridor of brilliant orange gates, surrounded by a still relatively untouched forest, is a dreamlike scene worthy of a Kurosawa movie.

The *torii* gate is one of the great enigmas of Japan. The meaning of the name, that distinctive color, and the austere form—all have great stories behind them.

The name, *torii*, is unusual, and there is no consensus on what it actually means or from what it derives. The literal translation of the two characters used to write *torii* is "bird(s) exist," in other words, the place where birds reside. This probably derives from the mythology of Amaterasu, the Sun Goddess, one of the most important and central deities in the pantheon of Shintō *kami*. There is an incident described in the *Kojiki*, the Records of Ancient Matters, in which Amaterasu was sorely abused by her brother, Susanoo. The rascal flayed a living horse and threw it into her weaving hall, and then pooped on her throne. Livid, Amaterasu escaped from the earthly plain into a cave and, by doing so, pitched the world into darkness. She was tricked by the other gods into leaving the cave, and thereby bringing light back to the world, by encouraging some "long-crowing-birds" to do their thing. Those very vocal birds being chickens, you can imagine the racket they caused.

I think the logic here, although there rarely needs to be logic in any mythology, was that the crowing of chickens, or rather roosters, as the sun is about to rise was not a case of the birds being urged to crow by the rising sun but, in reverse, the sun being urged to rise by the crowing of the chickens. Those chickens, it would seem, somehow had the power to raise the sun with their magical voices. Inducing the "long-crowing-birds" to sing was thus an attempt to cause Amaterasu to arise and show herself. The "place where the birds reside" is, therefore, when broadly interpreted, a sacred place where the *kami* can be called forth, or more specifically, the entry to that sacred precinct. At some later date the name came to be applied to the gateway that stands at that point of entry. This is, to me, the most likely derivation of the name *torii*.

But what about that distinctive color?

The bright orange color of the *torii* gates at Fushimi Inari is truly awe-inspiring, a kind of visual electricity that flows in through the retina and sparks the mind awake. However, it is most likely not the traditional lacquerwork that was used in yesteryear but a less expensive and more convenient paint, probably a lead-oxide derivative called *ninuri*. Originally, in Japan and throughout the world, that brilliant red-orange was achieved not with the metal lead but by using the mineral cinnabar, composed of mercuric sulfide. The powder pigment derived from cinnabar is called vermilion, as is the color itself. The exact shade of vermilion can be adjusted by changing the combination of additives as well as by simply continuing to grind the crystals of the pigment. The finer and smaller the crystals become, the brighter the color is, as is the case with the vibrant orange that is used on shrines in Japan.

In ancient China, the color orange was seen, from a Taoist perspective, as the color of transformation. In India, among Hindus and Buddhists alike, the color was associated not with the color of the citrus fruit but with the pollen of the saffron flower, which was used to dye the robes of monks and holy men. For them, the orange hue was the color of illumination.

The use of vermilion in Japan, and the techniques of deriving it from cinnabar, came from China along with the importation of Buddhism in the sixth century. The color is clearly eye-catching and was used on Buddhist temples and later on Shintō shrines to set them apart from secular buildings. Having been made from mercuric sulfide, however, vermilion also worked as a natural preservative for the wood it was applied to. It is easy to guess that this preservative power could have been interpreted as some kind of magical or godlike influence, driving the evil spirit of putrefaction away.

But whether or not people believed the color symbolized transformation or illumination or the fending off of evil spirits, surely the one undeniable effect was simply sensory. In a world before chemical dyes were available in all the colors of the rainbow, in a world without the electric lights that create such stunningly luminous scenes as Akihabara in Tōkyō at night, when the color palette that people were surrounded with all their lives comprised nothing but the greens and browns of the natural world, imagine in that world a *torii* gate of the most shockingly brilliant orange. Imagine having a mind and a memory that had only been soaked in the subdued colors of a natural world and then walking that mind through a tunnel of a thousand vermilion gates. It is shocking now, but it must have been downright hallucinogenic then.

That's the story of the brilliant vermilion color associated with *torii* gates, but in truth, most *torii* gates throughout Japan are not painted vermilion. They're not painted at all. Some are made of stone, which is not painted because it doesn't need the protection against weathering, but most *torii* gates are simply made of plain, uncoated wood. Fushimi Inari is a huge destination for devotees and tourists alike, but the reality of most shrines across Japan is that they are small affairs, with no tourist visitation to speak of, tended by the local people as they have been for centuries. Everything about those shrines is simple and unadorned and reflective of the roots of the religion—reverence for the natural world. That focus on restrained design includes the architecture, the artifacts used during religious ceremonies, and the clothing worn by the priests and priestesses who attend them.

Travel anywhere throughout Japan and look across the landscape you are passing through, and you will see from time to time a huge tree or grove of trees towering above its surroundings. This may be at the bottom of a mountain where it meets the flat land of the valley, or in the middle of the flatland, surrounded by an expansive sweep of rice fields, or even in the middle of a city. Find those trees and, like the spires of cathedrals in Europe, or the tall pagodas and stupas of Buddhism in Asia, they will guide you unerringly to a shrine. And at the front of the shrine will be a *torii* gate. Always. Bright vermilion or, more likely, unpainted wood, it marks the boundary between profane and sacred. But why that distinctive shape to the gate? What does that mean?

The form of the *torii* gate, with its two upright posts and two cross-beams, the top one typically flared at the ends like upturned wings, is very distinctive, no question about it, but, in fact, the gate itself has no meaning at all. Not originally.

The religion that is now called Shintō, the Way of the Gods, is based on the precept that there are numerous *kami*, or god spirits, in the natural world, and that those *kami* can be appealed to or appeased by performing certain ritual ceremonies of prayer or acts of cleansing that revolve around the use of fire or water. Before there was anything like shrine architecture, these rituals took place at points in nature that were perceived to be spiritually alive. It could have been at a waterfall, or a particularly grand old tree, or even a huge boulder that jutted out of the earth in an energetic way. The way that these sacred elements were marked to symbolize their importance was simple and elegant. A rope made of rice straw was tied around them. That's all. The rope is called a *shimenawa*. The word is written in various ways. One translates as "sign rope," another as "attention connecting rope," but, while the word *nawa* certainly means "rope," the word *shime* really means "to bind," so I like to think of the word as meaning the "binding rope."

The act of binding is an important one in ancient cultures. If you lived in a time before towns and villages, when people walked the land in tribes much the way other animals moved in herds or packs or flocks, you would become attuned to the imprints left by all those animals. It was a matter of survival. Hoof prints, paw prints, broken branches, scratched bark, chewed leaves, all these were clues to understanding what you were sharing the landscape with. Was it something you could

eat, or something that could eat you? Among all those marks
that animals could leave behind, only humans could tie a knot.
Even something as simple as twisting some tall grasses into a
knot was akin to screaming out in the landscape, Here Be
Humans! The power of the binding of plant fibers cannot be
understated, and that is why the simple act of wrapping a tree
or a boulder with a straw rope would be such a powerfully symbolic act. Günter Nitschke wrote extensively about this in his
seminal paper "Shime: Binding/Unbinding."

The simple rope wrapped around a tree or boulder was
later used in a larger scale to define not just a sacred object but
an entire sacred space. By surrounding an area with a rice straw
rope, that area became signified as otherworldly, a precinct that
sat somewhere between the mortal plain and that of the *kami*. If
you visit a small shrine in the country, or find one of the sacred
objects out in the forest that is still tended to by local people, the
shimenawa used will be a slender, roughly made length of rice-
straw rope, a simple thing that is remade after each annual harvest. If you go to a major shrine, however, one that is important
historically and culturally and has, because of that, become an
epicenter of human activity, then the *shimenawa* will be much
larger. Just as country chapels in Europe evolved into massive
urban cathedrals, so too do the major shrines in Japan have
different scales of architecture and religious ornaments. The
shimenawa that hangs under the eaves of the *kaguraden*, sacred
dance hall, of Izumo Taisha, purportedly Japan's oldest shrine, is
forty feet long and weighs over four tons. That huge, muscular

shimenawa doesn't make the *kaguraden* any more sacred than a slender rice straw rope would, but it sure looks impressive.

Not far from the massive Izumo Taisha shrine is a much smaller shrine called Kamosu Jinja. The shrine is smaller but also ancient, claiming to be the oldest extant example of shrine architecture in Japan. Next to that very old main shrine building is a series of smaller shrines, and then an unusual arrangement in which two branches of the *sakaki* tree have been cut from the local mountain and inserted into the soil next to each other. The *sakaki* tree, the name of which is written with a character that contains the glyphs for both tree and god, is a broadleafed evergreen tree that has become symbolic of everlasting life. The local parishioners who care for the shrine, who as a group are called the *ujiko*, will cut two new branches to replace the old ones in an annual ritual. The branches, each twice as tall as a person, are inserted into the ground and surrounded by a slatted bamboo fence. In front of that arrangement, to mark the area as sacred, there is a *shimenawa*, but it is held up in the air at about head height so that a person can duck under it and gain access to the sacred precinct. The frame holding the *shimenawa* up is made of two upright posts, just slender natural logs with the bark still on. These are simply planted into the ground and a cross-piece of bamboo is lashed onto them at the top. The species of the posts is not important; in fact, when I visited last the two posts were from different trees: an oak called *konara* and a mountain cherry called *yamazakura*.

That is the origin of the *torii* gate. Just a couple of posts stuck in the ground with a length of bamboo tied at the top, the purpose of which was to hold up the *shimenawa*. That's it.

The only thing of symbolic importance in that arrangement is the *shimenawa*. But *shimenawa* are made of rice straw, and they decompose readily. The structure that holds up the *shimenawa* is made of wood, which lasts longer. In later eras, it was painted wood or stone, and that lasts even longer still. As the support structures grew increasingly well built and more elegantly designed, and because the *shimenawa* was not always faithfully replaced due to the vagaries of time, the element that signified entry into the scared space, which originally was the rope, came to be the structure that held the rope. The *torii*, once just a lowly scaffolding, had become elevated to the status of sacred gateway.

If you travel around Japan, you will find shrines everywhere, countryside or city. In most cases, you are welcome to enter, and if you do, as you pass the *torii* gate, the custom among Japanese people is to bow toward the shrine that lies further in. Next time you do so, as you stand there on the threshold, think about the name and the color and the form of the gate you stand beneath, and more than anything, about the long history that it represents.

little secrets everywhere

The world is filled with hidden messages,
if we only know how to look

In a small town in the north country, in front of a liquor shop, I came across a strange image. Parked out in front, waiting for someone who was across the street in the bookstore, I was just looking around, a little bored, a little curious. One of the windows of the liquor shop was swung open at an angle, by chance just the right angle to reflect the bright red vending machine next to it. The reflection appeared to fit in the window like a painting: a bright red Coca-Cola sign cut out and inserted into the frame. It held there, taut and bright, like sunset on still water, and I found myself entranced and watchful. Then I began to notice something else, something that made no sense. There was, if my eyes were not deceiving me, a small shrine floating in the Coca Cola graphic. It was a gossamer thing, yet once seen it became increasingly clear, and as it came into focus, the two images fused. A small wooden shrine, like a little roofed house with a neat, twisted-straw rope hung across the front pillars, hovering within the red and white swirls of the soda graphic. I leaned a little out the window of my car and peered harder, hand like a hat brim over my eyes to shield them from the summer sun. I could make out the small stairs of the shrine, the tiny white bowls that held offerings of rice and sake, a small porcelain bottle with a clipping of a *sakaki* branch, an evergreen tree that features in Shintō rituals. Two images fused: one ancient, local, born of nature and the cycles of the seasons, and the other the most vivid symbol of modern, global commercialism conceivable.

It dawned on me, not long into this investigation, that the shrine was in the darkened room inside the window, on the back wall of the liquor shop. It is typical for people to keep a shrine in their homes or their businesses to pray for the health and safety of the people within. The glass was of the type that is treated to be slightly reflective. The whole thing just a mirror game. A trick of the eyes it turns out. And yet, I think, perhaps not. In that single view, the layered images of the old and the new, the reverential and the rapacious, there was a message, the kind of message that stops you in your tracks and makes you think about things. How we live our lives. What we consider important.

The world holds these hidden messages by the bagful. It's just a question of knowing how to look. Or, rather, to be willing to look. To be open to their revelations.

The poets of Japan have always been interested in nature, and in hidden messages. In particular, the poems called *tanka*, which means "short poem," almost always have some aspect of nature as their central theme. Tanka poetry follows a specific meter. There are five short sections, often written as five separate lines in English, which follow a pattern of a set number of sound-beats, something akin to syllables in English, 5/7/5 in the first half of the poem and 7/7 in the second, for a total of 31 sound-beats. The themes of the poem are wide ranging and, as mentioned, are almost always something gleaned from nature. Take, for instance, the ariso, the wild and rough rocky seashore battered by waves; the numa, a wetland that fills with water but has no apparent outflow; tsuyu, which is the dew that settles on the leaves of plants on cold mornings; or hagi, a large-growing shrub with pendulous branches that is covered with small pink blossoms in autumn. The poets pick one of these elements to weave into their poem. The result is a poem that points the reader toward a certain aspect of the natural world and, at the same time, functions allegorically to invite reflection on the human condition.

As one example, in the eighth-century anthology of poems called the Man'yōshū is a poem that incorporates an image of a numa. A wetland, such as a numa, may have a stream or streams running into it, but there may be no apparent outflow, because the water is simply percolating down into the ground. The allegory drawn from this is one of pooling without release, which in the poem relates to both a certain aspect of the natural world, the numa, and also to the feelings of a person who is in love but cannot express their feelings, which build up with no release.

MAN'YŌSHŪ 3022

yukue nami, komoreru onu no, shitamoi ni, ware zo monomou,
kono koro no aida
anxious thoughts
    of my secret love
swamp me these days
      pooling with no release — like the hidden waters
    of this little marsh

The poem has its own beauty, the sound of the words being spoken or chanted as they vibrate the air inside your inner ear. The poem also works as a pointer toward nature, to remind us of well-known aspects of the natural world or alert us to previously unnoticed aspects, like the flow of water in the wetlands. And then the poem comes full circle as it makes us reflect on our own lives. Three stages of understanding that are built into almost every *tanka* poem.

This sort of allegory can be found, not just in poetry, but in every corner of the world because every little thing in nature is always in some way, in fact in an uncountable number of ways, related to something else. Nothing stands alone, all things are connected to other things and are, therefore, by their very nature, allegorical. In the words of Thomas Merton, "All things are symbolic by their very nature, and all talk of something beyond themselves."

In traditional *karesansui* gardens, the white gravel raked into parallel lines to symbolize waves in water came from a local river, which was carrying away each and every day the shed skin of the mountain it flowed out of, so that, oddly, those tiny pieces of stone in the garden, which are intended to represent water, are in fact decomposed mountains.

The frog crushed flat on the road in front of my house, which remains in a permanent jump, arms and legs flung out in all directions as it was at the moment it was run over by a car or a truck, and then run over again and again and baked in the noonday sun until it became a paper-thin print of a jumping frog pasted onto the road, now speaks to me every day of frogs and cars and the massive churning society of man that tramples everything in its way.

The little boy walking, still unsteadily, down the sidewalk pushing ahead of him a wheeled toy of a character from a recent anime that is all the rage now, followed at a pace or two by a man in a suit who matches him step for step while somewhat neglecting his fatherly duties of oversight as he stares intently into the screen of his cellphone, head bent to his work like a mendicant monk, followed at a pace or two himself by an old man with a brimmed hat set firmly on his head, puffing with unusual delight on a cigarette that he has been warned more than once not to smoke, all three walking in sync like ducks in a row, each clutching their own addiction.

The world does not present these symbols and metaphors and allegories for the purpose of being viewed as if it had some kind of inherent thespianism built into its DNA, but there they are nonetheless. The world is full of them, little secrets everywhere, just waiting to be found.

the gift of flowers

*Thoughts on the fundamental, ancient
reason why we offer flowers as gifts*

The scene is a subway station, in a place and time when pub-
lic transportation is not well maintained and the stations are
home to litter and graffiti and the occasional drunk or two
sleeping on a cardboard bed. In the dark and fetid channel
below the platform where the trains run, water pools along
the tracks, quickened only by the occasional rat searching for a
tossed sandwich or the remnants of a bag of chips. An express
train comes barreling through, the sheer weight of the train
rattling the walls, the clattering roar of the wheels replacing
all other sounds, sparks snapping and cracking from the third
rail as if it is Shango or Thor or Yopaat or any one of the
other thunder gods that is leaping through. The air pressure
in the tunnel rises, then surges, momentarily lifting all the
scattered litter, sending it in whirlpools along the dirty platform. The train disappears into the opposite tunnel, its fiery

eyes winking as they recede into the darkness, and the air settles in its wake.

In the midst of all this grime and squealing power, inexplicably, I see on the other platform across the tracks, a young woman in a pretty white dress. She looks conspicuously out of place, but she does not act it, appearing comfortable with her surroundings or perhaps just oblivious. Held in both of her hands, before her chest like an offering, is a bouquet of flowers. Not the usual roses or lilies, these seem to be wildflowers that she might have just picked herself in a meadow somewhere. She has some more of them woven into her long-braided hair. Slowly she rocks on her heels, her eyes fixed on the tunnel that will bring the train she is waiting for. Does she realize that it is Thor that comes for her? Or Zeus?

Why do we do that? Give flowers to our lovers or lovers-to-be.

I used to hike and camp a lot when I was young and lived in the northeast where the Appalachian Mountains come to be named the Adirondacks, Catskills, and Green Mountains. There is an art to understanding where to make a campsite. If possible, it should be near a source of water: a spring, a river, or a lake. You will need to drink and cook and wash, all of which require water. So that's number one. Having a source of firewood close at hand is helpful, though in the northeast the forest is so littered with fallen branches that there is always more than enough to find with little work. The spot should be close to water but not so close that a sudden rain might swamp you.

Likewise, if it is on the slope of a mountain, it should be a rise or crest on the slope, not a valley where an evening's rain might gather and come sluicing down to wash you away.

When we camped, we were not living off the land—we humped most of our food in on our backs—but I came to understand just a little bit about what life would have been like for the earliest peoples who did live off the land. First of all, before people rode in carts, before they rode horses, they walked everywhere. Since time began and our simianic ancestors shambled their way out of that great southern continent, we have been walking the land. Living off what it provides to us. And when you live off the land, you walk the land in cycles, moving with the seasons, going round and round between known points, seeking food, and water, and shelter. And as you travel, as you walk down a mountain and through a meadow and along a river down to the sea and back up to the mountain again, you build up in your mind a map of the land you have traversed.

For a main shelter you'll choose a high point, maybe a flat spot on a cliff that has a fine view of the valley below. Perhaps there is a cave that is naturally protected from the quick approach of predators. Or worse yet, from bands of other humans. Along the valley bottom, ideally, there is a river with many bends and deep pools. The water is clear and fresh, the pools are filled with sweetfish. At the base of a hill is an outcropping of chert that has broken down into a long slide of broken shards that will make excellent tools. And back around the other side of the hill is a meadow where deer and rabbits graze. Each of those places goes into the map in your mind so that as you look out over the land you can sense, there is water, and there are rabbits and deer, and over there, good stones for tools.

As you are walking about with your tribe, scuffling for grubs, digging tubers where you find them, sipping water from the stream, there will come a day when you will see a blaze of color across the meadow. Sniffing the air you find it smells sweet, so you meander over to investigate. The trees there are covered with masses of delicate little flowers. You pluck one and taste it. Nothing to speak of in the way of food, so you meander off and forget about it. But just by chance, in your endless perambulations, you come back to that very same spot a month or two later. This time the trees are covered not with pink flowers but with hundreds and hundreds of fat cherries. The nimble ones in your tribe climb the trees and eat their fill, throwing more down to those who wait on the ground.

Over time the people of the tribe begin to put two and two together. Flowers turn into food, they realize, and so you learn to remember flowers when you see them. You also learn that there is no point in walking over to them when you see them. They're just flowers. Instead, you put the spot in your mental map and return sometime later, knowing you'll find food there. Over time, you and all of your tribe come to know this basic and most important fact for survival—flowers are signs of future food. Groves of nut trees, apples, pears, buckwheat growing in drifts in a meadow, sunchoke along the banks of a river, blackberries at the edge of the forest, each of these will flower and your tribe will note the place in their collective memory as a spot to visit again in the near future. And when they go, they will eat well. The ancient walkers learned that flowers symbolize a promise of food.

In time flowers also began to be used as a message from one human to another. You like a man, so break off the branch of apple tree in flower, or collect a bouquet of bright yellow sunchoke flowers, and give it to him. In doing that, by giving those flowers, you say I will bring you food in the future. I will care for you. I like you, please like me back. Flowers are the ancient signal from one human to another that suggests you are offering to protect and care for them. It's built into our ancient tribal memory, if not our DNA.

The air pressure in the tunnel rises and a southbound train comes rattling out, screeching to a stop in front of the platform where the woman waits with her flowers. The doors open loudly and, after a short minute, close again. There is a hissing and an electric humming, then a loud clank as the train lurches into motion once more. It passes down into the dark tunnel, red eyes winking as it disappears. The young woman did not get on the train. She stands there still, now looking at the ground by her feet, disheartened. Then, just like in the movies, a motion catches her eye and she lifts her head to see, at the far end of the platform, a young man in his Sunday best, hat tossed jauntily to the side of his head. He holds in his hand a single red rose. He smiles. She smiles back. He walks toward her in measured steps.

She steps lightly, almost girlishly, toward him, eyes fluttering between him and the floor. At arm's length they stop. He thrusts his rose out somewhat awkwardly. She takes it and, in the same motion, passes him her wildflowers. They step forward and, as if pushing through the tall grasses of an ancient meadow, they lean in between the bundled flowers and kiss.

there is no such thing as art

A reflection on art, craftsmanship, and aesthetics

In that corner of the city, many galleries had been opened in what had once been small factories and warehouses. The façades remained as they were, all dingy brick and stone, but the insides of each had been uniformly reborn as bright white chapels to that great religion that gathers the well-heeled and the paint-splattered alike. I happened upon one at a time when it was empty. No wine and cheese was being offered so no crowd had gathered. No whales were inside with their checkbooks so the air was not buzzing with the prospect of a major sale. I had the place to myself. There were various works in a retrospective of contemporary art: large-scale photos and paintings and sculptures of all genera and species. I meandered past an aquarium in which a viewer peering in sees only themself peering back, passed a painting of an enormous vagina or was it an enormous painting of an ordinary vagina, through a dark room

with little lights like fireflies appearing in response to my movement, and ended up in an empty room at the very back of the
gallery. Off to the side of the room, at the base of one of the
fourteen-foot-high bright-white walls, was a crumpled piece of
paper. It caught my eye and I sidled over closer to it, glancing
down and away, behind me and back at the paper, like a crow
approaching some roadkill. I stared at the paper for some time,
taking it seriously, pensively even, then looked around for a
label that would identify the piece. Sometimes, labels are put
on the wall near the work and sometimes, when the artist or
gallerist dislikes the distraction or limiting effect of labels, they
are placed at the entrance or nowhere at all. There was none to
be seen. Mmm. What was it, this paper? Art or litter? Frankly, I
couldn't tell.

What is art anyway?

I thought about that for some time, years really, and
through that process identified three aspects of art that helped
me to see it in a new light.

The first of these is a basic definition of what art is. This is
in no way the end-all definition of what art is. No such thing
exists, nor should it. As with any thing that can be viewed subjectively, that *needs* to be viewed subjectively, the beauty is that
there are endless answers, and any one person can believe many
of them at the same time. No harm in that. But I like my answer
for what it reveals about the potentiality of art.

There is a tale I have heard told, or read in a book somewhere, about the artist Henry Moore. He, as you must know, was
a sculptor who worked most famously in large bronze castings,

or rather, large castings were made of the work he did. The process began with the carving of smaller plaster maquettes. One day, he was carving a form, something shell-like, with a hollow part to it that was getting deeper and deeper as he worked on it, and darker and darker as it fell further into its own shadow. Then, quite suddenly, as he continued to work away at the bottom of the declivity, his chisel broke through to the other side, and out of nowhere, there in the darkness of the hollow, was a spot of bright light. Bam! Everything changed for him at that moment, an epiphany that would remain in the final work.

That is art.

I think we can all remember as children being given a sheet of white paper and some fingerpaints. You dip a digit into the red jar and draw a quick line across the page and suddenly, where there had been nothing, there is now something. Emboldened, you put two fingers in the green and squiggle down across the red line and now there is motion on the page. A dab of yellow, a smudge of blue, a smear of orange, a handprint in black, and with each mark, the scene in front of you changes and grows. Godlike, you are creating something from emptiness, and it is nothing short of mind-blowing, each step along the way an epiphany worthy of Pygmalion. Though your eyes are alight, there is no smile on your face, the whole process being so serious and gripping. This act of creation consumes you and it will not end until the entire page has turned into one big brown mess, at which point perhaps the spell breaks and you can breathe again.

That is art.

There is no art in the gallery I had visited, none in any museum or private collection, because art is an emotion not a thing. It is the series of epiphanies and disillusionments we feel during the process of creation. This thing we call art, it is here, inside us, not out there, in the world. The things we have made through that creative process, as a result of that art experience, are what we call "works of art," and that is a perfect expression because it reveals that the object, be it a painting or a sculpture or what have you, is simply a manufactured outcome of the art experience. Collateral creation. The real art happened inside the artist.

When we see those works in galleries or museums or on the walls of our own homes, it is possible to sense what the artist was feeling as they made the work, as they were experiencing *art*, but it is a tangential understanding. Maybe even an incorrect one, a mistaken guess at what the artist was experiencing. I really don't see that as a problem. They are separate things: The experience of art for a person in the process of creation and the experience of works of art in another setting are cousins, not twins.

Andy Goldsworthy is famous for his works of art made through the subtle manipulation of natural materials. A ring of broken stones or a graduated field of colored leaves. He is also famous for his privacy, making these works far from the prying eyes of other people. If it wasn't for his excellent photographs, much of his work would be made and lost to time, weathering and disappearing without anyone knowing about them. His own experience of being there in the grassy field or on a frozen river would remain within him, but the work itself would be lost. There are, of course, a hundred thousand other people of all ages and backgrounds, out there each day diddling with the things of nature they find in forest and field, piling rocks by a river or making patterns in sand, not with any intent of attention or publicity, simply because they seek the pleasant experience of creation. Simply to feel the art. Although they likely will not have the perseverance or design sense that makes Goldsworthy's work so stunning, they will likely experience some similar epiphanies and disillusionments in the process.

There is a paradigm shift that takes place when one comes to see art as an emotional experience instead of the object produced by that experience. Of course, for visitors to galleries or museums, the way they look at works of art changes when they realize they are viewing only some remnant artifact, akin to a strange object found by archeologists at the site of a sacred ritual. But the greatest shift is for artists themselves who begin to remember that sense of childhood wonder; freed from the need to produce a *thing*, they can once more simply revel in the act of creating it.

●

The second thing that occurred to me in my musings about art revolves around craftsmanship and, specifically, the recent shift in the art world away from it. The particular skills that require years of training to achieve, whether it is how to blend paints or use a brush or a chisel, are seen as distractions from the "concept," which is thought to be the only important aspect of the work. Sol LeWitt wrote, "In conceptual art the idea or the concept is the most important aspect of the work ... the execution is a perfunctory affair."

I couldn't disagree more.

There are many possible conceptual groundings for artwork. One artist might be focusing on gender issues while another is interested in time and space. If someone is addressing matters of social justice, someone else might be interested in environmental issues. Mysticism, politics, religion, symbolism, dreams, identity, they're all possibilities. To the degree that a person thinks about any of these concepts, when they work through in their minds the various pros and cons, the historical background, the interconnections that enliven the concept, to that degree the person thinking these thoughts is an intellectual or a philosopher. It is the work of those people to mull things over, to use the mind to cleave through ideas and reveal their inner workings.

However, the minute they try to convey what they have been thinking about in words on paper, if that is the medium they choose, they enter the realm of the writer, and that is a different arena entirely. There are people who simply have a knack with words, who can convey meaning clearly and, at the same time, present their thoughts in such a way that moves the reader. And it is this ability to skillfully manipulate words—it is their craftsmanship—that makes them a good writer.

If that intellectual/philosopher tries to communicate their thoughts not in words on paper but in spoken words they become an orator, and if the words are set to music they become a singer, and in each of those cases, it is the very way they speak or sing—that complex calculus of tone and timbre and breath and passion—that will have the ability to seduce a listener. It is their particular craftsmanship with voiced words that gives them the ability to propel their message into the world.

And even as this is true of words, so too is it true of paintings or sculptures or dance. Someone comes across a work of art created by a person who is highly skilled in the craft of their art, and it stops them in their tracks, causes them to lean in, to look or listen closer, makes it so they can't help but want to stay where they are and be with the work longer. To listen to the music, to read the passage over and over again, to touch the fibers, stroke the stone or steel, or watch the bodies moving through space. They have been caught by the magic of the work, and the artist has succeeded. The concept of a work of art is important, yes, in many cases vital, and yet it is a hollow thing unless expressed in such a way that can captivate its audience, and that kind of magnetism or gravity is induced only through craft.

※

The last thought that came from my long pondering of the inherent meaning of art concerns aesthetics. In common parlance, "aesthetics" is used to refer to certain superficial aspects of a work of art that are thought to be very much in opposition to the deeper inner meanings that artwork may contain. However, I have come to realize that aesthetics are more than that. Much more. They are not just those effete notions related to beauty and taste. Aesthetics are those aspects of a work of art that, by their very nature, affect any or all of the five senses and in doing so cause an innate bodily reaction. Aesthetics are those aspects of the work that reach in through the sensory organs and manipulate the very fibers of the body: heart rate, breathing, sympathetic nerve activity, endocrine response, capillary dilation, endorphin release, and all the other primordial systems the human body has built into it to cope with changes in its environment.

If, on a given day, a person is made to stand in a small room which is darkly lit, bitterly cold, filled with sharp, jagged objects, matted with what looks like dried blood and hair and reeking of waste and decay, how would they react? If on another day, the same person is put in a room that is light and airy, pleasantly warm, filled with soft, handwoven objects, and redolent with the scent of freshly baked bread or bouquets of jasmine and honeysuckle, how would they react to that? Surely, it goes without saying, their reactions to those two spaces will be entirely different.

These overwrought examples are presented simply to lay the groundwork for the idea that, since the world reaches into our minds through our bodily senses, a person who intentionally makes a work of art for other people to interact with must consider how that object will play on the senses of those people. It is the skillful manipulation of sensory markers, the control of the aesthetics of a work of art, that can result in the seduction of one's audience, and it is that moment of enthrallment that is the key to creating a powerful work of art.

confluences

*Living beings that exist so closely to one
another as to have become one*

In the summer, just as the sweltering heat peaks and the city air stills, thickening toward torpidity, I leave the city with my family for the mountains. There, we spend a few weeks of cool bliss in a cabin on a wooded hillside that slopes steeply toward a deep lake. Just beyond the door of the cabin is a dirt path that leads down through the trees. The soil is volcanic, moist and black. The path is narrow and shaded, overhung by high branches, encroached upon by grasses and ferns and low, spreading bamboo, close, cool, and lit from within with green. In rare places, the forest canopy opens to the sun, but for the most part it remains closed around the path, a narrow band of soil meandering darkly through dappled light and fading into foliage at every turn.

I come here to escape the heat, to mingle with friends, to dream. I walk through tunnels of green light that have no end, as if the walking itself would lead somewhere. Not to a place but to an understanding. And so it does.

And so it does.

Climbing the steep stairs that lead up from the hollow to the cabin I find a snake draped across the walkway, an *aodaisho* as long as my outstretched arms, green-brown, slender as a garden hose. It looks at me and flicks its tongue, then slithers away into the forest. I watch, entranced. Snakes. The old story. Mesmerize and capture. For me, though, it's not their unblinking eyes that attracts, it's the way they move, gliding across the ground as if drawn by an invisible string, proceeding forward with no apparent mechanism, the minor fluctuations that propel them invisible to the eye.

The snake winds its way up the slope, through beds of fallen brown leaves, over scattered twigs, moving nothing, making no sound, progressing as if magically. It flows up the slope and disappears behind an old stump half concealed behind the pendulous branches of a large shrub that grows beside my cabin. The stump is old, its bark long since fallen away. What remains looks soft. The flat top, thickly covered with delicate moss like a bright green cap. One small fern grows out from the corner. I poke at the pithy, orange wood with a stick and find it riddled with holes. Termites.

Sitting on the stone steps and looking at the stump, I can't help but imagine the hundreds of termites that must be crawling around inside it, chewing their way deep down through its roots beneath the soil. I like termites. That is to say, I like them

conceptually. The way they symbolize a certain intense confluence within nature.

I pull the stick out and find a termite clinging to the end
of it. When I knock it off, it scurries blindly around the stone
stair. When we look at a termite we see an insect. A singular,
separate living organism, entirely self-contained. And yet, it is
not. To begin with, no solitary termites exist. They are entirely
social creatures. So I cannot say, pointing at the little squirm-
ing bug, "This is a termite," any more than we could pluck
some cells out of our own bodies, a strand of nerve ganglia or
a section of skin, and say, "Here goes a human." The individual
termite, neatly contained within its own exoskeleton, is not a
stand-alone unit. Instead, it is merely a small component of a
colony, a larger organism the parts of which are able to move
about independently. It's as if our internal organs were to each
sprout legs, go about their business during the day, and collect
again at night. Conceptually, we should see individual termites
that way because they are nothing without the whole, and if
they are nothing without the whole, then the whole is the true
entity.

Their societal structure is notable, but what really makes
termites an example of unity within nature is the fact that they
live in a unique symbiotic relationship. A perfect example of
mutualism. In order for termites to live, they must eat wood.
Ordinarily, cellulose, the basic component of wood, is completely indigestible, but termites, because of certain protozoa
that live inside their intestines, are able to process it. The two are

one—termite and protozoa—unable to survive without the other.

In that link between two separate beings—a link that is required, not happenstance—we touch on an important point that expands the meaning of what defines an organism. We find that some of the elements that cannot be extracted from the organism without disrupting its life, and are therefore essential to it as a life form, are not necessarily originally part of the organism itself. At times, they can include other life forms that were traditionally defined as separate organisms. The termite and the protozoa, and the colony that termites live in, can all be seen as a single living being.

There are many examples of mutualistic relationships in nature in which two life forms survive because of each other. The one we all know and see all the time would most likely be bees and flowers. Flowers reproduce through pollen, which could be carried by the wind to another flower of the right kind, but the chances of that go down exponentially with the distance from the source flower as the pollen disperses into the world. Along comes the bee that is only interested in stealing pollen to make honey. The flower loses a lot of pollen that way but that really doesn't matter because it makes far more than it really needs, and as a consolation, the bees take the pollen that sticks to their legs directly into another flower, very likely the right flower, and thereby act as pollinators.

Ants and aphids are another example of mutual benefit, one in which the ants end up farming aphids like a herd of Holsteins. The ants stroke the aphids with their antennae, which causes them to excrete a sugary liquid, quaintly called honeydew, that the ants collect as food. In return, the farmer ants end up playing the role of guard dogs, keeping predators that would eat more than the honeydew at bay. Likewise, the clownfish that lives among the tentacles of a sea anemone. Normally, the sting of those tentacles would kill any fish unwary enough to wander into them, but the clownfish has a layer of mucus covering its skin that protects it. The plus for the anemone is that the clownfish ends up protecting it by scaring off potential predators like the butterfly fish.

There are many such symbiotic relationships where two life forms benefit from the proximity of each other, but none can be so close and so integral as that of the one that we call lichen. Lichens are, in fact, not a single living organism, they are two—algae and fungi—living together in such a tight, mutualistic relationship that they appear to be a single entity. The fungi make up the structure and form. The algae are photosynthetic, so like tree leaves they can make energy from light. The fungi offer the body, the algae provide the food. These two entities are not just symbiotic, not just mutualistic, they are fused to the point of being inseparable. That's the way we should see termites. Not a solo operation, but a duo, bug and protozoa working together. A single, unified idea. An integral unit, the two parts of which cannot be separated and survive.

Humans have something along these lines going on as well and it is, of all things, the community of microbes that lives in our intestines, also known as gut flora. Like the protozoa in the termite, our gut flora helps us digest the food we consume. There is some disagreement whether this flora is passed on from mother to child in the womb or after the child is born, but the principle remains the same. This is not stuff born of our own DNA. We have been colonized by an alien species and don't even know it. In fact it is a host of alien species, an invading army of Biblical proportions. And now there is talk of a gut-brain axis—a symbiotic relationship between the gut flora and the central nervous system—and we find that a healthy development of gut flora results in a healthy state of mind and vice versa. We sit up here in our brain, looking out from the eyes, listening through the ears, and by "we" I mean the logical, condescending entity we think of as "ourselves," and that observational creature peers out into the world through those eyes and ears and thinks it is in control. We sit up here smugly under the impression that we run the show, and the whole time the subconscious brain and gut have been gossiping about us. Could we really be so oblivious?

I like the idea of these confluences, those points of intersection where things of the world merge and find a harmonic way of being together. It gives me hope for the rest of the world. The chloroplasts that make plants green and turn sunlight into chemical energy, as well as the mitochondria, that provide energy in the cells of animals, both of those were originally separate life forms. They started as bacteria that were engulfed within early one-celled creatures when life on this planet was still young. Chloroplasts and mitochondria exist symbiotically within almost all complex life forms, keeping their own DNA, yet plants cannot live without chloroplasts nor animals without mitochondria. And neither can you nor I. And, even as I use those pronouns, You and I, I cannot help but think that singular pronouns shouldn't exist all. Not for people, not for other living things, not for any thing. If "I" am nothing without the mitochondria thriving in my cells, if "I" am nothing without a jungle of microscopic flora in my gut, aren't "I" always "We"?

The termite colony will keep. I leave them to their stump dinner and head back up the hill to the cabin to find my own. Entering, the smell of vegetables roasting comes from the kitchen. I take a deep whiff and soak myself with the scent of garlic and olive oil. My son is carrying plates to the dinner table. I light a couple of candles. Food is carried out, wine poured. We sit down to eat. A small confluence of three.

wind in the trees

Understanding what trees are really made of

I find myself on the back porch of the cabin, watching the wind rise in the trees. I look first to the top of the tallest poplar. Poplar leaves are light and hang on to the twig they dangle from by a long thin stem, so they move at the subtlest suggestion. The lower trees and shrubs that fill the foreground, protected by the taller trees above, begin to flutter and wave only with a stronger wind, one with enough force to push down through the leaves of the woods. The cedars close to the house, with stiffer branches and needles for leaves, move only when the strongest wind blows down around the cabin.

Before I head down to the lake, I check the trees, and judge by them the temper of the day. A good day for sailing, a bad day for swimming, this and more can be read in the hollow outside my cabin, just by the motion of the leaves. An anemometer by the lakeside, though it might mark the wind speeds more accurately, could tell me no more about the mood of the day than I can see here from the back porch. In fact, much less. The anemometer would tell me the wind speed accurately but it wouldn't show the sky behind it, as the trees do, and hint therein its mood. It wouldn't have the light on the leaves that changes with the cloud cover, at times hard and deep-shadowed, at times soft and pale. It wouldn't have the distant sounds of thunder, the touch of air on skin, or a silhouette of birds casting overhead, going north or south as the season urges them to. What an instrument gains in precision it loses in scope, and while a battery of instruments might offer the needed volume and array of data, they wouldn't, inherently, offer information holistically. In that, the hollow near my cabin excels, and what's more, it offers that information with grace and beauty.

It is also possible to discern much more in the landscape than the weather. The ordinary things that surround us speak volumes because they describe, by their very nature, all things large and small. That is certainly true of these trees that surround the cabin, and all those in this forest, and all those around the world. In all the trees and the wind in them.

On one of my travels through the countryside of Japan I came across a torii gate, an elegant post and beam structure that marks the entry to the precincts of a Shintō shrine. The path through the torii gate led into the forest, as most if not all torii gates in the countryside do. Compelled as if called, I entered. The path soon came to a steep flight of stone steps at the top of which was a tiny shrine. Off to the side, another path continued up the hill and, after a short walk along it, I came upon an old man making *sumi*, the charcoal that was used in all manner of ways for daily life before homes came to be hooked up with electricity and gas. The rougher grades of *sumi* would be used for everything from cooking to heating—if you can call the *hibachi* a heater. In the West, the *hibachi* has become the name for a small Japanese-style barbeque, but in Japan the word *hibachi* refers to a fairly large round ceramic vessel, like a squat urn, that is filled with a fine ash on top of which *sumi* charcoal is burned. The *hibachi* would be placed next to an invited guest, or the owner of the house, or the eldest person in a room, and it had the effect of slightly warming one side of their chest and face, or taking the chill off their hands. It never had the power to heat a room, especially a room in a Japanese house, the design of which is inherently well ventilated (read drafty). Glowing *sumi* embers were also put into a ceramic box called an *anka* that would then be slipped into a *futon* before someone lay down to sleep and thereby warm it on a cold winter night.

The collier I met was deep in the process of pulling the *sumi* out of the kiln and was covered from head to toe in a dark gray dust from which his eyes peeked out at me. Once he got over the surprise of meeting someone on that trail where people rarely traveled, he was kind enough to show me the pieces he had made. Most of the sumi was of the sturdy kind, the rough lower-grade material that is the workhorse of the charcoal trade. The kind that is used for general heating and cooking. I didn't ask but was almost certain that in this particular man's house, even if he had electric and perhaps gas service, he still used charcoal for all the basic needs, probably all the bits and ends of what he made, whatever was left over after he had sold off all the good stuff in the city.

There was one pile set aside for finer material that he said was being saved for a tea master he knew who used the charcoal to heat water during the tea ceremony. The tea master would stop by once or twice a year to purchase the best of his *sumi*, and the old man mentioned, a tinge of sadness in his voice, that he thought when the venerable tea master passed on—for he is older even than me, he said, as an aside—there would be no one left to buy that finer grade of *sumi*.

Sumi is made from hardwood trees, often one or another variety of oak. *Ubame-gashi*, a kind of evergreen oak, is very popular for that use. The man I met was using *kunugi*, a kind of deciduous oak that has a very thick, notched, almost corklike bark. When *kunugi* is made into *sumi* carefully, the results are outstanding. To begin with, unlike the lower grade charcoals that use larger pieces of wood from the main trunk that have been split into smaller sections, the charcoal for the tea ceremony uses smaller branches. The character of the branch, the way it bends and twists, the texture of the bark, all remains evident in the final product. When you look at the cross-section of the wood, at the ends of a branch-turned-into-*sumi*, you can still see the corklike bark separately from the wood, and in the wood you can still make out the growth rings. The wood often splits radially from the center outward, in what's called "checking," making a pattern that is known as kikusumi or chrysanthemum charcoal.

The thing that impressed me so deeply about this finer grade of sumi made for the tea ceremony was how much the finished sumi looked like the original branch from the kunugi tree. It was almost the same size; there was only a little shrinkage. The texture of the bark, the growth rings, all were there exactly as in the original wood. The weight was a little lighter but not so much lighter than a fully dried branch. There were only a couple things that were different. One was that the density seemed to have changed so that the sound two pieces of sumi made when tapped against each other had become less wooden and more metallic. The other was that, unlike the original wood, the sumi was totally black. The heat of the kiln had driven out of the wood any remnant water and all the other volatile compounds such as hydrogen, oxygen, and methane, so that the kunugi branch had in effect been alchemized into an exact replica of itself, except this new form was simply pure carbon.

A tree is made mostly of cellulose. Cellulose is mostly made of carbon. Although trees grow in soil, the carbon they are made of is not drawn from the ground up into the tree in mineral form, it is pulled out of the air, split off from carbon dioxide. The chopping block where this task is performed is the leaf. The cleaver is chlorophyll. Air comes in through the porous surface of a leaf. Water is drawn up through fibrous channels from the roots. The two, air and water, meet in the leaf where chlorophyll will whack and chop, turning carbon dioxide and water into sugar, which in turn is made into cellulose. Of the carbon and hydrogen and oxygen that make up cellulose, as I found out at the *sumi* kiln, it is carbon that makes up the bulk of the form of the tree and that carbon comes from the air. Trees grow in soil but they are not made of it. They are crystallized wind, coagulated air.

When people talk about hearing the wind in the trees, I wonder if they realize how true that is. That the wind is not just passing through the trees and making that pleasant rustling sound in the leaves, it is actually turning into the trees. In the same way that baleen whales like the Humpback and the Blue eat by straining plankton out of seawater, trees strain carbon out of the air and incorporate it into their bodies. Next time you walk through a forest, pause for a moment to touch a tree and remember that it is no more than the wind made visible.

dissolving

*Watching the world decay into its
elemental parts and reassemble elsewhere
as something else*

One hot day this past summer, I was on top of the old cinder-block storehouse that sits at the back of my little garden, repairing the solar water heater, when I heard a distinct rasping sound coming from below. It sounded like something was being chewed away. Mice, I thought. Or shrews. Something like that must be gnawing away at part of the house. I wiped the sweat from my palms and, grabbing onto the heater, leaned over to look into the garden, but the angle, and fear of slipping into a fatal headfirst dive, prevented me from seeing what it was, so I bundled down the ladder to investigate.

The sound was clear and easy to locate but what it turned out to be was a surprise — the noise so loud, the object so little. A wasp. It was clinging to the old reed screen that curtains the cinderblock wall of my storage shed. Bit by bit, it was scraping away at the outer layer of wood, a shell-like coating that had separated from the reed over years of beating sun and winter frost. The wasp's sharp mandibles were working machine-like up the reed, scraping off rows of pulp. The hollow reed resonated the sound the way a bamboo flute might, amplifying it. The wasp took off, circled twice, then flew down toward the green *aoki* shrub in the garden, ducked under one of the broad leaves, and disappeared.

Later that day, having finished my chores, I was getting ready to take a shower when I noticed in the garden, hanging on to the sheltered underside of one of the leaves of the *aoki*, a wasp nest. Three wasps were working away at it, one on top, the other two on the sides. They had managed to build five or six egg chambers already, tiny translucent paper cones hanging upside down from a single, slender thread attached to the leaf. The cones were filled with a green light that had filtered down through the leaves above them. Wasps crawled over and around the cones like black-robed caretakers of an emerald palace.

Days passed, the wasp nest grew, its weight pulling gently on the leaf, so when a breeze slipped into the small garden that leaf would bob slower than the others as if the nest were anchoring it in the world. I sat down once and watched for an hour. The wasps traveled back and forth from the old reed screen countless times and were, I came to understand, deconstructing the reed screen in tiny incremental amounts and recreating it as a nest beneath the *aoki*. The body of the one becoming the body of the other. I imagined if I were to sit there watching the comings and goings of the wasps for long enough, the entire reed screen would slowly be erased from the world before my disbelieving eyes as, at the same time, the world became populated with veritable cities of nests. How long would it take? A hundred years? A thousand? Of course I won't stick around to watch but it's going on nonetheless, happening right there in my back garden for all to see. The subtle dissolving of the world.

My house is small and simply built. It is made of only two materials. Wood and soil. In the wood category are the cedar trees used for the posts and pine trees for the beams. The ceiling is made of very thin boards of clear cedar, as are the narrow slats that make up the frames of the sliding doors that separate all the rooms. The paper pasted on those doors—the translucent *shōji* and opaque *fusuma*—comes from the white inner bark of the *kōzo* and *mitsumata* shrubs. Slender *igusa* reeds were used to make the *tatami* mats. The lath within the walls is bamboo and the rope that ties the lath is made from rice straw. All of that wood was harvested from the hills and valleys surrounding Kyōto. The walls of the house, on the other hand, are made with a clay-based soil that is also gathered from the ground not far from the city. The wall starts with a rough and gritty layer pressed into the woven-bamboo lattice, then a finer middle coat is troweled onto that, and finally, there is a surface layer of clay that was chosen for its soft brown color. The roof of the house is made of wave-patterned tiles that are themselves also made from clay, a very fine clay harvested from the estuaries of rivers, or canals near old rice paddies, that have deep sedimentary deposits. Of course there is the glass in the windows, and the metal in the electric wires and the pipes for gas and water, but in reality these are but a small part of what makes this house what it is. In fact, in houses that were built more than a hundred years ago, houses that were for all intents and purposes the same as the one I live in, those more modern materials would not have been used at all. Basically, my house is made only of wood and soil, and much of that comes from the mountains and valleys that surround the city.

The house was not built by wasps, although that idea is incredibly appealing. I can envision a skyscraper being built by flocks of wasp-like robotic flying machines that gather materials on the ground in their semblant mandibles and fly up to deposit their loads layer by layer on a slowly emerging tower, creating a structure more akin to a vertical paper nest than to human architecture. No, my house was not built by wasps but it happens in the same way as a wasp's nest. The hands of hundreds if not thousands of laborers and craftspeople scrape away at the natural world—a bucket of clay here, a tree or a shrub there—and carry it all through their various workshops, then to this city, to this very street, and assemble it once again in a new form. The world dissolving in distant places and reappearing on this narrow lane as my house.

This process of the world being chewed away at and rebuilt in new ways can be seen only at some times, in certain places. A wasp's nest or a home of wood and clay being built out of pieces of the world that used to be other things. Volcanoes erupting and creating entirely new islands in the middle of previously empty seas. Acres of spring grass turning into vast herds of cows as you stand there watching them. But overwhelmingly, the process happens on a level so minute and delicate as to be far below our ability to perceive. If it weren't for the occasional earthquake, we wouldn't notice the slow creeping of the continental plates that gradually and deliberately thrust and buckle to form mountains. Seen, but unnoticed, drops of rain dissolve infinitesimal bits of the landscape and carry them away in rivers to become a part of a new landscape somewhere else. Air turns into trees. Trees turn into soil. Soil turns into earthworms, which turn into moles, which turn into foxes. The whole thing tumbles forward in a web of interconnected spirals, becoming and unbecoming without end.

The world is never still. Even at rest, its shaping continues, as if the very air was filled with a host of whirling blades, hard and honed beyond resistance, whittling away in nips and bites, meticulously and ceaselessly. Bend in. Listen close. Catch the hum. The frenetic drone of the blades pitting and tinking against their work. If you keep very still on a moonless night when the wind calms to nothing and the forest holds its breath, you will hear it. But only if you're still—truly still.

And even as the world dissolves before the blades, so too is it building up. In measures being kindled and in measures going out. Always. Everywhere. So the hum you hear on that calm night might not be the destructive blades after all, but instead the frenzied work of countless subtle fingers adding carefully to the whole, a dab here, a dab there, like wasps at their nests. With each moment the mountain shimmers, a little up, a little down—the city grows and decays. You too. Nothing is the same for a nanosecond.

unity

Moments of feeling at one with the world

It was a fine morning, the air cool, sunlight coming warmly at an angle from the east, casting everything in light and shadow, giving form to even the most insignificant pieces of the world. A pebble on the road, a bright red leaf still clinging to an almost barren cherry tree. Cycling to work, I dropped down off the road onto the broad banks of the river and headed south, passing under bridges from time to time, traveling along an excellent bike path used by few others that runs the length of the city, north to south, and carries me most of the way from home to office and back.

At some point, I passed a flock of gulls rooting for breadcrumbs that had been cast by someone down the stone embankment that runs along the river. There may have been as many as fifteen or twenty gulls, squawking and flapping as they competed for a morsel of breakfast. I heard them first, then saw them, their wings like white swords slicing at the air. Just as I rolled up alongside the flock, as I was about to pass them by, perhaps because of the sudden motion of my passing or the humming of my wheels, the entire flock launched into flight, lurching up from the riverbank in unison. We merged, the flock and I, traveling along that path in the same direction for just a second or two, and for that moment I was one of them, beating heavily toward freedom, wings closely audible, soft puffs of air felt on the skin of my face, then they wheeled off left and right, scattering before circling back to the breadcrumbs on the bank. It lasted but for a moment, yet now, so many years later as I write this, as I recall that very moment, I am once again lifted in soft flight, feeling the rippling air on my cheeks, and am enjoined to fly. The thrill of that moment is so clear, I need to take a few breaths to slow my heart. Even now. So many years later.

There are these moments when we feel, inexplicably, like we have stepped through a veil. Crossed over into another dimension. Not a different place—no, everything is still the same as it was. There is the river and the cherry trees that line the upper embankment. There is the flock of seagulls and the humming of the bicycle wheels. It is all as it was and yet, at that moment, I feel as if somehow I am part of it, not simply aware of everything but somehow dissolved into it. The wings of the gulls become my wings. There is an overwhelming sensation of lightness and freedom. The heart soars as I slip gladly out of my own skin and into the world.

It has been full-tilt lazy-summer mode this week, tucked away in the cabin by the lake. Swimming, walking narrow paths of black volcanic soil through the forest, taking midday naps. The back porch is the size of a small room. It has a roof but no walls to speak of, or rather only hip-height walls meant to stop the unwary from tumbling off the edge and down the hill. It is a good place to share meals, or read a book, or write. This morning I am writing. Just by chance, a small insect lands on the screen of my laptop. It looks like a dragonfly but more delicate and hairier like a housefly. The screen glows, luminous within its dark frame, casting the spindly legged creature in silhouette. The composite eyes are gray, the legs delicately bent, and there is a fuzzy puff at the end of its tail. I blow lightly across it. It doesn't move an iota.

A few days ago, I went with my family to a local play park where children spend the afternoon pretending to be ninja. I was leaning up against a fence, watching my son run though the gauntlet of an athletic course, when a yellow dragonfly came clattering into view. It landed on the fence, then flew away again. Circling back, it landed closer to me this time. I held out my hand, palm flat to the ground, index finger extended. The dragonfly flew off and came back once more, landing, of all places, right on the tip of my finger. I was frozen in place, afraid to move lest the spell of that moment be broken. For just a moment, though it seemed like a lifetime, we held that way, the dragonfly and I, then it popped its wings out, raised its tail and clattered off again. I thought it would be gone for good this time, but it circled and came back, landing once more on my finger. Falcon to trainer.

Staring deeply into its green ball eyes, eyes made up of hundreds of smaller eyes, I wondered, Is there someone in there? Have we met before? Are you coming to me on purpose or do you just mistake me, standing here so still and breathless, for a fence post? Once more it popped its wings out, flicked its tail up, then flew off and circled back, coming to my hand again. I felt like I had a puppy. Like we were pals, this bug and I. A strange excitement came over me, the thrill of being socketed into this creature, and through it, to its world. A world of pixelated colors and motions, blurred objects tracing across my field of view.

One of the boys stopped his ninja game and came over to me. He raised his hand up close to mine. Slowly, I lowered my finger to his. The dragonfly remained motionless, then flitted over to the boy's waiting finger. Like me before him, he was stunned, frozen to the spot. More freely honest than I, the amazement showed on his face, a broad smile creeping outward from his lips to encompass his crinkling nose and widening eyes. My joy and awe had remained inside me, though I wear it to this day. Even now, sitting here on the porch, writing, with another delicate insect settled on the screen of my computer. I reach out a finger. Slowly. And dare to hope.

·

Breakfast today, as every day, is out on the porch. The forest that surrounds the cabin is green to the point of insanity. Delirium viridis. It is all I can do to even think of eating. When the world is so alive, howling its verdancy at all who come before it, unabashed in its youth like naked children splashing gleefully at the shore, how is one to think let alone eat?

Somehow the meal is done, although it took three times as long as it would normally, the forest tugging at my senses unforgivingly, distracting me from the task at hand. It is only then that I see what, at first, I think is a hallucination. Like some kind of muscae volitantes, the hovering flies, those little transparent squiggles that drift before your eyes when you look at a clear sky. But this is not drifting or squiggling, it is dropping straight down and it is huge. And black. I pull back from the illusion, pressing against the back of my chair, and let my eyes focus. A spider. And not so big a spider at that. Just too close.

The spider drops to the arm of my chair, anchors the silken thread it had lowered itself on, and proceeds to climb back up the very thread it had dropped down on. Halfway up to the ceiling it stops and releases a gossamer thread, a thread so thin that it can only be seen against a dark background. I set my eye height to catch it against the wall and watch as the released thread drifts out horizontally. There is a very fine crinkling to the line, as if it had been somehow knitted to make it more buoyant. Although the breeze is so gentle that I can hardly feel it on the hairs of my skin, the spider uses the drifting air to cast its thread out and let it flow to the nearest surface. What the thread hits, it sticks to, in this case my hand. I have been volunteered as the second anchor. I hold still and play my part. The spider drops to the table, anchors another line and climbs back to the ceiling again, crawls over a short way and drops down again, this time to my laptop, where it releases another gossamer thread flowing out on the imperceptible wind. If I sit here for much longer, I will be bound hand and foot. The table, the ceiling, the computer, and I will fall into a confederation of the spider's planning. Enough is enough. I have things to do. I lift the little arachnid from its sturdiest thread and set it gently on the porch railing, expressing apologetic sentiments I doubt it appreciates.

These subtle moments of unity happen out of nowhere. Seagulls along the riverbank. A dragonfly landing on a finger. A spider stitching you into its web. I am of the opinion that those rare moments are what Zen Buddhists might call *satori*, enlightenment. Passing through the veil from the immediate moment of everyday life into a state of being that includes not only yourself, but all that is around you. All that ever was and ever will be.

If only that state of unity would stick, but it never does. As quickly and unexpectedly as it appears, it is gone. I am just about to get there, just about to pass into that excellent state of bliss and then, poof, there is nothing but the same river I pass every day. A dragonfly like so many others. A spider dangling from its own thread.

symmetry

The concept of symmetry from both ancient-mystic and contemporary-scientific points of view

---

The banks of the river I ride to work each morning have been shaped into neat tiers and the riverbed tended so that it is almost flat. Water control. The age-old urge. One autumn morning last year, one of those days when the air is clear and perfectly still, and the river lies flatly taut like a mirror, I came to a point where the flowing water fell over one of the many weirs that cross the flow. Seen from upstream, the mirror surface of the water just ended at that point, disappearing abruptly. The sky and clouds and trees along the opposite bank that were hanging upside down on the water surface, an inverse picture of the living world, simply vanished there. Just like that. As I drew closer, riding downriver from the north, I caught sight of a large gray heron flying upstream toward me. We approached the weir from opposite directions, the heron and I. It squawked loudly as if calling a warning to the world below that it was coming in for a landing. I stopped to watch. The large bird banked sharply, making a long, slow turn down to the water, its wings arched gracefully to the sides like broad gray outriggers. As it made its slow descent, I could see it reflected in the still water. There was one bird falling down through the air and another bird rising to meet it from the water below, their motions precisely in sync. They drew close to each other, bird to bird, one rising one falling, and at the very last possible moment, cupped their twinned wings like drag chutes and slowed, stretching their bony legs out toward each other, and touched toes as they came to rest, one upon the other.

The world craves symmetry.

Or, is it the mind?

The way human eyes and visual processing work, we are keyed into finding and appreciating symmetry. A well-balanced face, for instance, is considered to be beautiful. The thought behind this is that the balancing of facial features is itself somehow indicative of health and, therefore, of the possibility of reproductive success. It's always about sex, isn't it? So if we inherently see the world in ways that make us seek out symmetry, that make the acquisition of symmetry a pleasurable experience for us, then it follows that there will be a tendency for us to want to find symmetry in objects and systems. Do we find symmetry because we want to, or is it really there?

One obvious and undeniable example of symmetry is the human body; in truth, the bodies of most animals. The design of bodies always puts the sensory organs on the lead part of the animal, the part that faces toward the predominant direction of movement, for the obvious reason that the animal needs to sense the field ahead of it to a greater degree than the field behind it. The grasping appendages, if they have them, are situated in such a way that they can draw food into the mouth. No point in having hands or claws on your back that can snatch food but not feed it to you. And the symmetry we find in the external form of animals has developed simply because those bodies move forward through space, and that symmetry allows for balance along the axis of movement. Having a body with long legs on one side but not the other, or wings or fins or flippers for that matter, would put a big dent in the ability to move smoothly in one direction. And if the symmetry of bodies flows naturally from underlying needs, so too might the symmetry of other aspects of the natural world.

According to Taoist thought, in the very beginning, by which I mean the very very beginning before even the universe existed, there was a state of being called *wuji*, written with the two characters for "no extremities." *Wuji*, in other words, was a completely unified state within which there was no differentiation between things. No light or dark, no hot or cold, no up or down. At some point, in an instantaneous and cataclysmic event, *wuji* changed states into *taiji*, "extreme extremities," and from that change flowed all manner of stuff that makes up the universe as well as the systems that control it. In Taoist thought, prime among those systems are the paired principles of *yin* and *yang*. Yin is typically described as the receptive aspect and *yang* as the active one. Whereas these dualistic elements can be described in contrast to each other, light versus dark, sun versus moon, male versus female, the most important property of this concept in my mind is not the duality, but the interconnectivity. To begin with, *yin* and *yang* only exist in relationship to each other, and are therefore inextricably connected to each other, almost to the point where you could say they are one, or more to the point, two phases of one thing. Also, fundamental to the description of *yin* and *yang* is that one always contains a kernel of the other and is in fact always initiating and giving rise to the other. The idea that *yin* and *yang* are opposing elements at the opposite ends of a spectrum is only true in an instantaneous snapshot of their reality. The broader picture, the longer-term picture, shows that they are part of a system in constant flux and are only temporary apparitions of an underlying process.

Of course modern physics has long replaced the idea of *wuji* changing to *taiji* with the concept of the Big Bang, which is also described as a primordial unified state giving rise, more or less instantaneously, to the universe. Science has replaced *yin* and *yang* with other dualities such as matter and antimatter, positively and negatively charged atomic particles, and every action yielding an equal and opposite reaction. There are many examples, but the symmetries that I find myself always captivated by are the ephemeral ones, the poetic ones, the ones that I can't help but find in the world around me, like the graceful joining of a gray heron and its reflection in the waters of a still river.

There is the cyclical symmetry of the seasons, not a precise physical pairing and mimicry but a comforting understanding that the phases of the world will come around again. If the mountains are alive with new flowers, a time the Japanese call *yamawarau*, the laughing mountains, we know that in a year's time, after a hot summer and a hard winter, they will laugh again. If there is a drought or a deluge, in time there will come a righting of the scales and rains will once more come or stop as needed. There is an inherent balance to the world that is reliable and beautiful, but it is not a perfect balance because it is always in flux, always readjusting itself. It moves in the jittery and clumsy way of a person feeling their way across unknown terrain, because there is no great plan being followed, simply a constant, constant seeking to fill voids and balance energy while changing form from one thing to another. A simmering inconstant chaos in the nanoscale that somehow bubbles up into the delightful form of the world we see around us. A river through a city. A cluster of lonely clouds that seem to have lost their way. The fluid arc of a heron in flight, descending through autumn air to meet itself.

rivers of the mind

On the liquid state of the world and the mind

There is a river in the north country that meanders through a stretch of flatland, a rarity for that part of Japan which is known for its mountains. At one point it runs between *wasabi* farms on one side and a patch of forest on the other. The water is not deep, but it is crystal clear, the kind of water that makes you think that the little boat you are paddling is simply levitating above the river bed. Small fish, *masu* and *iwana*, gather in the shadow below the boat, their tails beating against the stream to hold themselves in place. Then a sudden movement, or perhaps the sound of the paddle, and the fish disappear like those vivid dreams that evaporate upon waking, leaving you to wonder if they had been there at all. I slip out of the boat and let my friend paddle it on as I drift downstream on the surface of that crystal water, floating aimlessly like a fallen leaf.

The bottom of the river is covered with long strands of

water-grass that wave and undulate languidly in the stream like Ophelia's long hair. I quiet my heart and breath, and let myself just float. No exertion. No focus. The minute currents that cause the grasses to meander back and forth slowly become perceptible. They don't move me as they do the grasses, I am not that light and supple, but I can feel those little seams of water sliding over my skin. The repetition becomes mesmerizing and I start to feel the stream as if is flowing, not over me, but through me, within me, as if the seventy percent of me that is water had been loosed and was flowing downstream with the rest of the river. It was somewhere along there, suspended in a dream of melting into the river, that it occurred to me why there is such a strong connection between water and life.

Solids are too fixed to become the basis of life. Their very stability does not allow for the necessary transfers that take place within organisms, even simple ones. Imagine a one-celled paramecium made of solid iron or quartz. In contrast, gases are too dispersed to be the foundation of life. They allow for transfers easily, but offer too little substance to become the essence of a living being. Liquids, on the other hand, offer the kind of density required for the development of an organism but also have the fluid nature that supports the various chemical and physical interactions from which life is born.

Of all the basic chemical elements on Earth, only two are liquid under the usual conditions that exist on the Earth's surface—air pressure, temperature, and so on. Those two are bromine and mercury. Both are rare and highly volatile. Of the commonly occurring molecules on Earth (carbon dioxide, quartz, water, etc.) only water is liquid, and it makes sense that the most commonly occurring liquid on Earth would turn out to be the basis of life here. Perhaps, on any given planet in the universe, the life forms that develop will always be based on the predominant liquid found there. It's tantalizing to imagine a planet so hot that sulfur is liquid, where there exists a multitude of lifeforms all colored yellow or deep red and smelling of rotten eggs. Or a planet so cold that nitrogen gas is liquid and great whale-like creatures swim in nitrous seas.

●

Rising behind my house is a mountain, one that stretches in a series of peaks all along the eastern side of the city. The entire thing is a huge block of granite. This particular granite contains quartz, feldspar, and mica, which are white, gray, and black, respectively. The result is a whitish stone that is speckled with gray and black in a salt and pepper fashion. Wherever the granite is exposed on the surface to the weather, it breaks down quite easily into gravel and sand, and when it rains, the gritty remains are carried away into rivers that leap down the steep valleys to the city below. The beautiful white sand that is raked with lines in the famous stone gardens of Kyōto is harvested from these rivers, or it was until recently when overharvesting forced the city government to ban its collection. Now most white sand used in gardens here is imported from China.

The mountain is typically thought of as a symbol of

solidity and permanence, and yet, if you look closely you can see it, there, in the rivers that flow down into the city, the mountain itself melting away like so much wax from a candle. This is the way of all things. Small parts come together and cling, forming a paramecium or a person, a mouse or a mountain, but at the same time that they are coming into being, so too are they breaking down. The mountain behind my house sloughs away in measured degrees every moment of every day, just like the river, ceaselessly changing. According to Plato, Heraclitus said that you cannot step into the same river twice, but just as true is that you cannot step onto the same mountain twice. That very thing we think of as the epitome of solidity, the glorious upright mountain, is more fluid than we think. Dōgen, the priest who founded the Sōtō school of Zen back in the thirteenth century, alluded to this in his *Mountain and Water Sutra*, which is a meditation on nature as a window onto the essence of Buddhist truth. At the opening of the sutra are the lines "The verdant mountains are always walking, the stone maiden gives birth at night." Dōgen may have been using the expression "the mountains are always walking" to refer to masters of Zen practice who sit in meditation as still as a mountain and yet who are also always adaptable to change and in that sense are fluid, or always walking, but I don't need to look that far to see it. The actual verdant mountain behind my house is always walking, literally, always creeping up under the thrust of tectonic plate movement, always dissolving away in the rain and running off in the rivers as sand. At night, you can hear boulders break off and tumble down the hillside as if the stone maiden of the mountain had given birth.

Rivers of water flow, but sand alone can also flow like a river, even without any water. In certain situations, when affected by the vibrations of an earthquake or when hurtling downhill during a landslide, sand will become fluid and flow like water. Even though the individual specks of granular material are solid — each minute grain of sand no more than a tiny boulder — when caused to move quickly, or when vibrated to the point that friction is overcome, they flow just like water would.

Lately I've been thinking that ideas are like that, too. Memories and memes, each individual idea is like a grain of sand, a mote of thought that gets passed through a social network by word of mouth or by text, and like the rivers of sand, those discrete ideas are carried along in a kind of liquid flow. They travel until they find a suitable mind to settle in, the way grains of sand settle out of water in quiet eddies or estuaries where the flow slows down. And just as sand settles and begins at once to form a layered sediment that, in time, may compress and become stone, so too do ideas settle in the minds of people and, over time, become solidified as memories. And also like a river, the very flow of which will erode what it passes through, so too do flows of new ideas intrude into our minds and wear away at and even replace the older sediment of thoughts that existed there.

I float in crystal waters by the *wasabi* farms, face turned up to a shock-blue sky, watching sunlight filter down through over-hanging branches, and even as the river draws me downstream, and flows over and around me, so too do I feel the lifetime of thoughts that have flowed into my heart and mind. Some sticking, some not. Some laid deeply within me as the bedrock of my identity and my understanding of the world. And others, even now as I float over water grasses like Ophelia's hair, are beginning to erode beneath the never-ending stream.

the last god

The mystical beauty and historical importance of mutations and accidental occurrences

I must admit it could have been just the heat, or the intense light. Lying there on the sand with the sun as mean as it's ever been, hurling itself down on the world furiously, I watched through my all-but-closed eyes as the once white glow shattered into rainbow starbursts. I felt like I was seeing something astounding. Not a hallucination but a glimpse through the veil into what lies behind. In the mind-searing light there was a story being told.

The First God, the great one, shapes souls quickly, with an easy and subtle hand, and sets them floating down toward earth in numbers so great they look like rivers of soft light. They have the glow of things just made—scooped chunks of primordial plasma. She is fast with her work but not particular. Details are not her business. These she leaves to her court, through which the new souls must pass on their way down. As the souls pass these lesser Gods, each in turn has their way with her work. The God of Need, thousand-armed, always grasping, her hall filled with infinite desires. The God of Power, whose rooms echo with her constant howls like the night winds across these battered shores. The God of Efficiency, who moves little and only when needed but who cuts deepest and with least compassion. In that way, the souls pass through all the halls of the lesser Gods and their Consorts and Consultants, whittled bit by bit, added to and taken from, cleaved then fused, kneaded and set to rise, again and again, until each God has had their turn, and then, and only then, do the souls float lightly into the hall of the Last God. Some call her the God of Malice, some say the God of Blessings, others the God of Serendipity, but in fact she has no name and lives alone. No other God will deign to speak to her and none can divine her work. She is, if nothing else, fickle. As each new soul comes floating by she gives it a gift, but the gifts are, as is all her work, beyond comprehension. She bends to each soul in turn and touches it lightly. Loosens an atom here, adds a curl of flesh there, a subtle twist of green where leaf meets stem, a hole in a heart, some extra feathers on a tail already seven feet long, a blue spot at the base of the spine, a stunted nerve. And then, having made them each her own, she lets them go, for better or worse.

The First God you may call Solis, pouring out the photons that energize the world at its most fundamental level and allow for all life. The other minor Gods could include Chlorophyll, who changes those photons into chemical energy, and Enzymes or any of the other busy bees of the micro world, who act as catalysts to reshape reactions. And the Last God? Why not call her Mutation? Sure. The one who just cannot leave things be. The one who steps in and throws a pebble into the gears, or swipes a screw from where there should be one, and stands back with a grin on her face as she waits and watches for the outcome, shrugging off the failures and winking at the successes. Anyway, that's how I imagined her as I lay there, my mind half-roasted by the midday sun.

What does it say about the world that, at the very heart of things, life moves forward because of error, that we stand on the shoulders of an incalculable number of small mistakes that turned out to be brilliant in the end? What does it say about our societies, which favor in so many ways those people who do everything correctly, when in truth so many of our advancements have come from the accidental and the unintended? When we ourselves, the very bodies we inhabit in this life, are compilations of millennia of minor mistakes in DNA that have led, accidently yet inexorably, to the form we have today.

A shadow passes over my all-but-closed eyes and I wink one open just long enough to catch the shape of a gull sailing overhead to join a flock that has gathered above the sea cliffs where the ocean breeze lofts upward like an invisible elevator. By canting their wings at just the right angle, the birds are able to fall down through the air at exactly the same rate as the warm moist air is pulling them upward and, as a result, go neither up nor down but manage to hover in place for hours on end with only the slightest effort. They slip from side to side, growing closer and further apart as the minutes pass, but other than that, they remain in place as if floating, weightlessly. I have seen the same thing on a ferry traveling from island to island, above which gulls and terns use the wind cresting over the ship as a static wave, surfing on that invisible hill and letting the ship do all the work, traveling with ease over great distances of water and only banking away when they reach their destination. What cascade of errors led to just that shape of body, just that cross-section of wing, just that density and flexibility of feathers, that inexplicably allows those birds to ride currents in the air that we can't even see?

A small prickling on my toe calls me to find a crab trying to make its way back to the water. What complex and serendipitous series of small mutations led to this little creature being able to breathe both underwater and out in the air. Its delicate feathery gills are tucked in behind the joints where its legs meet its shelled body. Gills work fine in water but would collapse out in the air and become useless. Through millennia of the Last God's touches, some parts of the gills have been hardened by conversion into sclerotin and thereby have become stiff enough not to collapse. Also, there is the way the crab can bubble water out of those joints so that it introduces oxygen into the water and passes it over the gills to allow them to function even when not totally immersed, as if it had worked out a means of carrying the sea along with it as it walks up onto the shore. What an elegant and precise creation, the end result of how many failures, how many crabs with insufficient gills that died trying and whose shattered shells now mingle with the quartz and feldspar crystals in the sand.

And what about you? That little thickening of the skin that you've noticed on your hands, or the odd shape of your incisors, or that annoying inability to filter sensory input that keeps you forever jittery, or the shape of your red blood cells, or the heightened activity of your mitochondria. Are any or all of those the very qualities that will prove essential and become standard issue for all humans in ten thousand years? Who's to say?

The sun has passed behind some clouds over the ocean. The hallucination of bursting sunlight and a pantheon of gods has passed, leaving only a nasty sunburn and a nagging sense that every answer lies in the crooked and flawed corners of the world.

paths

On paths that exist in the world — some human, some not

The path that leads through the woods down to the lake is always in half-shadow, the canopy of leaves above it greedy of the sunlight that falls on them. The soil of the path is black and always moist. Mossed and glistening. In these woods, the paths have a garden-like appearance, subdued and calming. That quality undoubtedly stems from a balance that has been struck between user and place, and not from maintenance, which in this community is of the rough-annual and not the meticulous-daily kind. The banked sides of the path are thick with ferns and slender grasses that lean over in pendulous arcs toward the legs of people walking through. Some of the ferns are still just beginning to unfold, and those fiddleheads can be seen here and there among the already leafed-out ferns, appearing as tight spirals within a sea of overlapping fronds. The tip of one fern, all but unfurled from what was once a tight spiral, has formed a small circle at the end, the way the seated Buddha is depicted with forefinger and thumb lightly touching each other in the mudra of enlightenment.

The ground is covered in places with small nuts that have dropped from the broad-leaved trees above and lay scattered on the moss. In other places, where sunlight filters down through the canopy of leaves more strongly, there grows a single-leafed herb called *fuki*, the stem of which makes good eating. Nuts and *fuki*. If you know where to look, the forest is full of food.

Startled by my tromping feet, frogs pop across the path, escaping into the leafy cover on the sides. They are lean and sharp-nosed, like little brown darts, whizzing back and forth about my knees. Where the path breaks out into a patch of sun, instead of frogs it's grasshoppers that scatter by the handful, jumping this way and that with a click and a whir. This path is alive. Beetles, butterflies, mice, and moths, all skedaddling into forest as I approach. We meet here each day, briefly, on this lake-bound path, and yet it is not their path. It is mine. Or ours. We two-legged creatures who amble up and down it each day. Unlike a road, which is a purpose-made thing, an intentionally constructed surface, a path is only a record of passage. A memory of all the feet that have traveled along it. Use a path a lot and it stays packed and clear. Stop using it, and it returns to the forest as quickly as you can say gone and forgotten.

None of these small creatures follow the packed earth path for long. They merely cross it like the moles that tunnel underneath, leaving soft mounds of earth across the path every few feet. A snake basks in the sun along one stretch but slithers into the cool grass when I come, hissing threateningly once or twice before leaving. Dragonflies seem to follow the linear clearing of the path for a short while but soon shoot up and away in a new direction. I use this path every day, but there are a million other paths in the forest and, of that multitude, this is the only one I can see.

If I were smaller, much smaller, and had a much more refined sense of smell, one that was tuned to the aromatics of pheromones, perhaps then I could sense the paths left by ants, those trails that let them follow one another through the jungle we call groundcover. If I were a hungry salamander, perhaps I could follow the slick paths that are left in the wake of a slug as it eases its way across the forest floor. If I had the eyes and mind for it, perhaps I could see the paths left by deer or bear, the trails of scat, the broken stems, the clawed or chewed bark. And if I were larger, much larger, and could stand as tall as the clouds, or if I could fly, and in that way look down from far above, perhaps I could see the paths left by rivers. Not just the ones they follow now, but the ones they used to follow and have left behind to fill in with eons of dust and debris. If I could look down from that far above, perhaps the paths of energy that run through solid rock would become apparent, the sheer force lifting and shattering the landscape in such a way as to leave paths of destruction and creation that form the very land we live in. Yes, the world is full of paths that lie hidden in plain sight, unseen but for the realization of how to look.

As the path nears the lake, it drops to a low point next to a small bog. No trees grow there, it is too wet for them. Instead, the hollow is filled with reeds and tall grasses. The tops of many of the reeds hold each a dragonfly, their wings held out to the sides like solar panels, transparent and marked with a black dot. And from somewhere in the bog, or from a tree on the edge of it, comes the song of an *uguisu*, a warbler not much bigger than my thumb whose dulcet call sounds amplified, as high and pure and clear as a flute blown with confidence.

I turn at the bog to follow another path, one that leads along the lakeshore, in between the pebbled beach and the forest. There are many paths in this forest to be explored, and I think I have walked all of the ones made by people at one point or another, but there are other paths in Japan only a few of which I have traveled that are long and deep and exist only in the heart. Whereas Westerners tend to say that something exists only in the mind, to refer to things that have no physical presence, Japanese tend to say only in the heart. There is no traditional word for mind, not in the Western sense of what a mind is. Or, rather, in a situation when a Japanese person wants to say mind, they would touch their chest and say, *kokoro*, or heart. Not the blood-pumping organ called heart, that is *shinzō*, but the heart/mind that is felt to reside in the chest.

These paths that I am referring to, the ones that don't exist in the physical sense, are, of course, the paths of the arts—both the martial arts and the fine arts. The names used to refer to these arts all contain the suffix *dō*, which means path or way.

Among the martial arts are *jūdō*, the gentle way; *aikidō*, the way of harmonious spirit; *kendō*, the way of the sword; and *kyūdō*, the way of the bow. Among the fine arts are *sadō*, the way of tea; *kadō*, the way of the flowers; *kōdō*, the way of incense; and *shodō*, the way of the brush.

In each of these art paths, even though physical objects are obviously involved—a bow or a brush—the path itself is not of the material world. It is an inward path, a journey one takes via the medium of the art to attain a spiritual awakening. The art itself is the vehicle, the path taken is something that exists only within the heart of the practitioner. In *kyūdō* for instance, an arrow is shot at a target, yes, but the hitting of that target is not the main point. The practitioner is not critiqued by their *sensei* on how close to the center of the target they get, but on how the whole process of shooting was carried out, what is called the *shagyō*. The feet are placed in a strong position, the bow is lifted above the head, the hands drop and spread outward stretching the bowstring away from the bow, and then, when the string is pulled as taut as it can be, the practitioner waits. Eyes are fixed on the target, unblinking, as they send their spirit out to it, creating a path that the arrow will simply fly through, like an invisible tube in the air. The practitioner waits just a moment more and then releases, but even then the process is not over. They wait for just a moment more in a state of *zanshin*, residual spirit, and then and only then, do they lower the bow and step away.

In *kadō*, the arrangement of flowers is the central vehicle of the art, but there is an important step that is not directly related to the arrangement itself, which reveals clearly how kadō is more than simply the art of arranging flowers. In fact, this step has to do not with the flowers that are placed in the vase but with those that are left over, unused. When the process begins, the practitioner will have before them some seasonal flowers, or grasses, or even stems from a shrub or tree. Carefully, they plot out the arrangement, snipping at unwanted parts of the plants and slipping them into a vase. In the case of flowers that are being arranged for a tea ceremony, chabana, there may only be a single flower used in the arrangement, but whether it is a flamboyant contemporary arrangement or a hyper-simple one for tea, the plant materials that are left over are not thrown away. Instead, they are carefully gathered and tied into neat bundles in a process that resembles the preparations of a sacred offering. When all the remnants have been neatly bound, they are not put into a garbage pail but, ideally, are taken someplace where they can be composted and returned to nature. It is this act that speaks most clearly of the attention to, and respect for, the living things that are being used as the vehicle to travel on the path of flowers.

I walk this dark soil path by the lake, sharing it with the many small lives I meet along the way, taught something by each of them as I go, and consider that this most pedestrian act is also a way, in and of itself. Let's call it ryūdō. The Way of Wandering.

dream garden

The essential, philosophical meaning of
a garden

As happens on certain days, when the air is cool and a pool of sunlight warms the spot where I have been sitting, I find myself drifting into that delightful somnolence of which dreams are born. Breathing slows, eyelids soften, and the world is seen not as it is but as it might be. Looking down from a high place in one of the hills that surround the city, in this dream I find that the city I know so well has been utterly destroyed and become instead one of those post-apocalyptic scenes known so well from films and photos of urban warzones. What had once been a thriving place, home to 150 million souls, is now a gray wasteland of half-shattered buildings and ruined streets. The grid pattern that the city had been built around is still oddly visible through the mounds of rubble and remnant structures, the original idealism of the city's layout somehow showing through the chaos that replaced it. There I see the broad avenue

I used to ride my bicycle along to work, and over there the cross street I used to take to go shopping. Could that pile of debris be the co-op I belonged to? As I search across the wasteland, trying to find some vestige of the life I once had, I notice a dot of green within the urban desert. In all that vast expanse of dust and debris, there grows a single, massive tree.

Walking down what used to be called a street, the ankle-deep dust lifting in clouds behind me with each step, I move cautiously, jumping at each sound, unsure of what lies around each corner. A flock of crows is noisily fighting each other for some scrap of food they have found. So all life has not been eradicated. Of course. How could that possibly be? On a planet that has withstood massive extinction after extinction, what is more dependable than the fact that some life will rebound and occupy the new epoch? And even as I think this, as I see the toad that the crows are tearing into pieces, I see as well some moss on the northern faces of broken walls, tufts of grasses peeking out from piles of rubble, the tracks of many small feet in the thick layer of dust that covers everything. And there, across the rubble hillocks that mark the remains of once great buildings, the billowing tree.

Seen closer, the tree rises above a courtyard, the enclosing wall of which was cobbled together with shards of concrete stacked twice as tall as a person stands. The only gate through the wall is made from a sheet of rusted steel, lashed onto a post with old aluminum powerlines. On the north side of the courtyard are the remains of a seven-story building that used to be a hotel. The whole façade that faces south onto the courtyard had been cleaved off by some terrible blast, the edges now as jagged and frayed as torn cardboard. Whatever windows it once had are long gone, revealing the honeycombed interiors of each floor. A toilet here, a shower there, a painting still hung crookedly on one of the walls. But the old rooms are not empty, no, far from it. On each floor, plants are growing or I should say, are being grown, for it looks like a vertical farm. I can see fruit trees, berry bushes, what looks like a rice paddy, and vegetable patches. Someone is hard at work there.

A push on the gate and it swings open. There is no bolt or lock. One wonders why the door is even needed then. Entering I find a garden. The massive old tree billows up above it all, casting a shadow across a large pond filled with lotus plants. People in boats are fishing with nets for the carp and eels that they keep there. Around the edges, tucked up against the enclosing walls are cottages that must be their homes and workshops, and on one side of the pond is a gathering area with a shed that seems to be an outdoor kitchen of some sort. Many people have gathered for their midday meal, taking food from a communal sideboard and joining the others at one of the long tables. The people are of all sorts, or rather of no sort at all, impossible to tell where in the order of the old world they may have come from. Dark and pale and in-betweens. Raven-haired and flaxen and every shade of brown. Tall, short, and middling. Eyes of every color imaginable.

Someone sees me standing in the entrance and calls out.

The others stop eating and turn to look. For a moment we hang that way in the uncertain space of first meetings, then the man who called out waves me over with a smile. A child of no more than eight teeters out to greet me, still clutching her cup, and takes me by the hand to guide me to the table she had been sitting at. We eat, they talk. The language seems familiar, a word here a phrase there, but the whole is utterly incomprehensible to me. Music is played and a song or two sung, everyone joining in on the chorus. I cannot catch the words. No matter. I smile and clap my hands along with the others.

Someone is calling my name. The meal was so good I must have fallen asleep I think, but no. That is not it. My eyes flutter open to find my hiking companion standing in front of me, hands on hips, amazed that I could have dozed off with such a view to look at. I shake my head to clear it, smiling shyly. There in the valley below, the old city still lives and breathes as it always was. I get up, still half dazed, and trip along the path after her. As we walk I try to tell her of the garden I had dreamed of, an Eden-like place within the desolation. It wasn't there, she says pointing to the city. It was here, tapping me on my chest.

Not out there. Here. Within.

Arcadia where Pan and his nymphs cavorted. Shambhala, the Tibetan Place of Peace, the Land of Radiant Spirits. El Dorado near Lake Guatavita, ruled over by The Gilded One. Avalon, the Island of Apples, where Excalibur was forged. Gulliver's Laputa, hovering above the land of Balnibarbi. Fiddler's Green, the seaman's dreamland of everlasting mirth and never-ending fiddle music. Nirvana, where the liberation from *saṃsāra* yields perfect happiness and quietude. Valhalla, the Hall of the Slain, where warriors who die in combat go to be at Odin's side. And, yes, of course Eden, within which grows the Tree of Life.

History is filled with many stories of idyllic places, places that are held apart from the day-to-day lives of the people who tell the stories, of the people who hear them being told, and yet, although those places are always described as being far away—across a sea, over a mountain range—at the same time they exist right here within us. The telling of the story imprints within our hearts and minds the very possibility of such a place, and though few if any of us will ever attain passage to the actual paradise, all of us can share in it just by thinking of it. Just by dreaming.

Of all these idyllic lands, the one that speaks most clearly to me of this true, inner garden is the *beyul* of Tibetan Buddhism. *Beyul* are paradisiacal lands that lie hidden in plain sight, secreted beyond a mountain pass that no one has traversed before, or perhaps existing in something akin to a parallel universe that remains unseen until it is revealed and opened by a spiritual guide, a *tertön*, who has uncovered the required hidden text. Like the *beyul*, the true garden does not exist out there in the world, it is not made of things living or mute, not something we walk into physically to enjoy. It is nothing more, and nothing less, than an idea that we keep close within us. An idyllic place that we can return to in our dreams.

wheels turning

The dimension-shifting magic of the potter's wheel

A friend asked me to join him for coffee the other day. We met in a downtown cafe and were talking about this and that, idle things. Most of what we said I don't remember, but somehow we got on the subject of seeking truth, and he said something that stuck with me. He was talking about the way people develop awareness and said that he thought there were three distinct stages, the first being the satisfaction of physical needs: food, water, clothing, shelter, sex. The second stage, he contended, was the aesthetic. Stabilizing sources of food, through improved hunting or agricultural techniques, leads to cuisine: the skills of cooking, flavoring, presentation, and consumption. Crude outfits of skin or plant fiber develop into fashion, the look of the clothing, and what it expresses about the wearer, becoming a function as important as physical protection. Likewise, shelter becomes architecture, not only protecting those

within from their environment but also expressing the sentiments of the society that created them. Sex for the sole purpose
of reproduction is replaced by more complex practices, devel-
oping into forms as diverse as perfumed and flowered courting
to sadomasochism. And, of course, many other arts that are not
linked to basic physical needs come into existence at this point:
painting, sculpture, music, theater, and so on.

The third stage he described was the awareness of things
spiritual. Having satisfied one's physical needs, and then continued to plunder the aesthetic possibilities of the world, one
develops a thirst for something deeper. A need to explore those
aspects of being that are not dependent on the temporal body.

That talk over coffee came back to me in a roundabout way
many years later. It was early summer; I was watching wasps
build their nest in the back garden. I closed my eyes, just listening to the drone as they took off and landed at the nest. Then
the sound of the wasps seemed to rise in volume and shift in
tenor and placement, coming now not from the garden in front
of me but from the other side of the house. The new sound,
louder and deeper than the first, entered my thoughts as a flight
of many bees, a swarm buzzing up through the house, and the
hairs on my neck tingled. But it was rhythmic and cyclical, not
really the sound of bees, a kind of electric hum, and then I had
to laugh. I realized it was not a wasp attack at all but the quiet
droning of the potter's wheel in my wife's studio. I went to see
what she was working on.

On the other side of the house from the tiny garden is the

studio. Like the garden it is small, crammed with blocks of raw clay and finished works drying on shelves, offering room for little more than one person at a time. But, nevertheless, from time to time I have sat and watched as she throws cups and bowls. The work is mesmerizing. Of course the circular motion of the wheel is slightly hypnotic, and I'm sure that part of what I feel is physical, a pleasant form of dizziness, and yet I can't help but feel there is something more to it than that. A certain primal power resting within the wheel itself. That day, when she left to run an errand, I sat down, grabbed a hunk of clay, and set it on the wheel.

With the machine switched on and clutch engaged, the clay turned in slow, methodic circles, slightly off-center, wobbling around like a drunk on the dance floor. Shaping it into a smooth mound, I nudged it toward center and slowly it balanced itself, the motor droning and pulsing like a quiet breathing. The revelation that followed, which led me to remember my friend's thoughts on the stages toward spiritual enlightenment, happened in clear steps, each one urging me to the next.

It went like this.

The motor droned, the clay revolved, the green light of the garden reflecting off the slick, spinning hump. I began to fool around—what better way to happen upon things? On a nearby shelf was a box filled with potter's tools. I took a small bamboo stick that was sharpened at one end like a meat skewer and pressed the point into the wet clay. As the clay turned a line drew out, encircling the clay and closing on itself again.

The sharp tip of the twig was, more or less, just a single point. Theoretically, non-dimensional. Pushed into the spinning clay, however, it drew a line, a thing that is one-dimensional. Point to line; non-dimension to one dimension.

Zero to one. Now what?

Next, I took from the tool box an old piece of hacksaw blade that my wife uses to texture surfaces and pressed it to the wet clay. As the clay turned, a broad band of roughened clay stretched out across the surface. The blade, itself a line, had drawn out an area. One dimension drawn out into two.

One to two. I began to see where this was going and looked for my next tool, but what would be the two-dimensional that could become the three-dimensional? Of course. The clay itself. I pushed the tips of my fingers slowly into the top of the revolving clay, the way I had seen my wife do many times before, and though the result was not like what she accomplishes, the idea was the same. The slight depression became a hollow, the hollow a cup-shape until I had managed to pull up a crude, high-rimmed bowl. The walls of the bowl—a two-dimensional surface if cut out and laid flat—here formed a three-dimensional vessel.

Two dimensions had been spiraled up into three. This is great I thought. What next. Three to four? Space to Time? But how?

It took me some time to come to that. In fact it wasn't until the pots my wife had been working on were dried, fired, and we were unloading them from the kiln, still warm and crackling from cooling glazes, that it dawned on me. Some of the bowls had a thick covering of white slip on the outside. The slip had been applied with a coarse brush of bamboo twigs as the bowl turned, upside down on the wheel. The patterns of the slip ran around the bowl, wavering up and down like currents in a river. I could sense the motion of her hands, the subtle twists of her wrist. I could see it. Right there. Her experience of making the piece, the very timing of her movements, remained in the work, crystalized forever by the heat of the fire. So there it was. The wheel had captured time as well.

So clay can jump dimensions. The turning wheel adds, through its motion, one extra dimension to the work. A point becomes a line, a line becomes a surface, surface becomes space, space captures time. OK. So how do we do the same thing? How do we jump from Material to Aesthetic to Spiritual? What "turning wheel" do we lay ourselves against to spin us out into another level of perception?

For me, it is clear. Walk through green-lit paths lined with ferns and delicate white wild flowers, past crystal waters that reflect the tops of distant volcanoes. Sit watching wasps build their nest out of a dissolved essence that a few seconds before was a screen made of lake reeds. Drift in rivers of cool mountain water that elicit other rivers of drifting thoughts. Sit next to a courtyard garden so small as to defy the name and watch an old stump decompose and grow at the same time. These are the wheels against which I lay myself knowing that they will carry me beyond what I have already come to know.

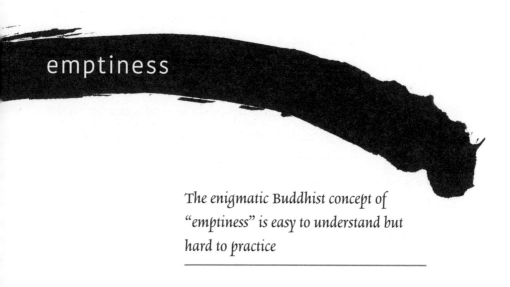

emptiness

The enigmatic Buddhist concept of "emptiness" is easy to understand but hard to practice

The pine trees here grow tall, in shapes that are almost like long tubes or what a gardener would call columnar. Of course, they do not grow that way naturally, they are shaped with scissors and saws, but it is unlike the way any other pine trees are shaped in the gardens of Japan. And that is because this is not a garden. It is a temple.

The tall and lanky form of the pine trees here is called *tera-sukashi* or temple pruning. They have taken on that form over the years because traditionally the maintenance of the trees in this temple was not performed by gardeners who were trained in the art of pruning but by young acolytes who were training to become Zen priests. In the past, there were many such young men who came in the hopes of entering the priesthood, and so there were always lots of hands in these temples to help with the care of the grounds. No need to hire a gardener. The young acolytes were simply sent up the tree and told to cut the branches off as far out as they could reach, the result being a naturally columnar shape.

I enjoy coming here just to walk around the sprawling temple grounds and see the many parts and pieces that make it up. Alongside where the pine trees grow is the central core of the temple. It contains several large buildings that are laid out in a formal Chinese style along an axis. From the outside heading in there is first an outer gate, *sanmon*, then a Buddha hall, *butsuden*, a prayer hall, *hattō*, and finally the residence of the head priest, *hōjō*. Around that central axis are randomly laid out sub-temples, *tatchū*, which are all but hidden behind their tall clay walls and elegant entry gates. Between the sub-temples are narrow roads that have been paved with stone. The work of paving was done over the centuries on an as-needed basis, so that it has both a sense of purpose and an organic randomness to its design. There are the beautiful interiors to the temples themselves, although few are open to visitors. And, of course, there are the enigmatic *karesansui* gardens that are found within the confines of walled temples, simple arrangements of stones and sand and moss that speak volumes more than their limited palettes would suggest possible. The pines and the architecture and the gardens—I enjoy all those aspects of the physical spaces of the Zen temples, but the most important aspect of Zen is not in the forms but in the practice, and one core of that practice is the concept of emptiness.

Volumes have been written about emptiness. It sounds almost comical, that so much should be written about a concept called emptiness, and yet there it is. The descriptions of Emptiness present it as an ephemeral, ethereal concept that is impossible to express in mere words, even as oh-so-many words are written about it. But the idea that emptiness is an illusory concept that is difficult to conceive of is not the way I see it. For me, the concept of emptiness is in fact straightforward and easy to understand. It is not the meaning of emptiness but the practice of emptiness that is the real challenge.

A main tenet of Buddhist thought regarding the nature of reality is that all things are in constant flux and that all the things of the world—the people and the plants, the stones and the seas—come into being through a complex web of interactions and causations. At the same time, those same things are also being broken down by another complex web of interactions and causations. Arising into existence and being extinguished from that existence at the same time. Always. Always. Ever-changing. This process is called "dependent arising" because no thing comes into existence in and of itself but instead is dependent on those endless webs of interconnections.

The difficulty in understanding the meaning of emptiness came about like this. If you want to explain the nature of reality, why things are the way they are, you could say that all existence is dependent on a web of interconnections. If you were to put things in reverse, and express what the nature of reality is not, you would say that there is no independent existence.

However, instead of saying that the world has *no* independent existence, it was decided in the distant past to say that the world is *empty* of independent existence. That's where the word "emptiness" comes in. The world is empty of independent existence.

It's a terrible way to express things and the root of endless confusion. This is clear if you look at what's happening with a different example. Let's say that I have a bowl of soup and I tell you the soup is piping hot. That is an expression in the affirmative of what the soup *is*. Piping hot. If instead I express it in the negative, and tell you what the soup *is not*, I would say the soup is not cold. This is true, but it is not so effective a means of describing things because when you say the soup is not cold, it could be piping hot but it could also be just plain old hot or lukewarm or room temperature or even cool. So, saying that the soup is not cold is not as clear as saying it is piping hot. But if I go one step further and, instead of saying the soup is "not cold," I simply say the soup is "not," well of course you have no idea what I mean. If I say the soup is "empty of coldness," there is some meaning to that description though not as good as saying piping hot, but if I say the soup is "empty," of course you have no idea what I am talking about.

As already mentioned, the nature of reality is that all existence is dependent on a web of interconnections. That could be described, in reverse, in the negative, as being empty of independent existence. Taking that a step further, if I just say that the nature of reality is that things are empty, of course you have no idea what that is supposed to mean. How could you? However, when you realize that the word "emptiness" is just a symbol, a stand-in expression for a larger concept, which is that all existence is dependent on a web of interconnections, then everything starts to make sense. If every time you come across the word "emptiness" in a Buddhist text, you substitute in your mind the phrase "all existence is dependent on a web of interconnections," everything becomes clear.

Take for instance a core line of the Heart Sutra:

shiki soku ze ku, ku soku ze shiki
Form is Emptiness and Emptiness is Form.

The word "form" refers to all of the things of the world—the aforementioned people, plants, stones, and seas. If you make the substitution I suggested, then that phrase from the Heart Sutra reads, "form is dependent on a web of interconnections and the web of interconnections causes all forms."

This idea of seeing the world, not as being made up of independent objects but as a system of holistically interconnected, mutually dependent entities, is so important because from that particular point of view flow all manner of enlightened understandings. To begin with it jibes perfectly with a contemporary scientific understanding of the world, whether you are looking from an ecological standpoint at the massively complex relationships between organisms and their environments, or looking at the carbon cycle that traces the flow of carbon through the air, earth, water, and life forms, or looking at the kind of fundamental interconnectivity that is expressed by quantum entanglement. I don't think there is any scientific field that doesn't agree that the world is massively interconnected. Although many of the world's religions find themselves at odds with scientific thought because it challenges some of their basic tenets such as the way they describe the creation of the planet Earth and the development of life on it, the concept of emptiness is totally in sync with scientific thought and, in that way, is a truly contemporary mindset.

Also from the concept of emptiness naturally flows ideas of environmental awareness and social justice, because the selfishness that lies at the root of environmental degradation and social injustice is not supported by a mindset that is based on the inherent interconnectivity of all things.

The hard part, as I mentioned at the outset, lies not in understanding what emptiness is—that is pretty straightforward, I think you would agree—but in attempting to embody that mindset in our daily lives. To foster what might be called an empty heart or an empty mind. To truly see the world as it exists with its infinitely layered connections.

A temple cat appears from under the veranda. It leaps up, lands on the wooden floorboards, realizes I am there and freezes, all in one fluid motion. When the cat sees that I am no threat, it plunks itself down on the veranda, lifts a leg, and proceeds to lick its crotch in a display I can only imagine is intentionally meant for my viewing.

I try to see the cat with an empty mind, to truly see it not as simply a cat, but as the sum total of the array of interconnections it embodies. You are what you eat goes for cats too,

I think, and as I can see by the little bowl in the corner of the *engawa*, this cat eats wet food, food that was brought by a truck from a distant factory where bits and pieces of leftover fish were processed along with godknowswhat into a semblance of a meaty meal, fish parts that came from a small coastal village where old wooden boats crowd the harbor at night and cast off into the unknown each morning before sunrise, including among them the fisherman who caught those very fish, who guides his boat across the cold northern waters crossing over shoals filled with kelp and clams and clots of shipwrecks out to deeper waters where the curved backs of whales trace graceful arcs through the moonlight and... Wait. Stop! I've just begun to look at the cat, for cryin' out loud, and have only begun to follow one stream of connections and already I'm lost down a rabbit hole. I haven't even started to try to calculate the number of oxygen atoms in the air that the cat breathes in, or the number of CO_2 molecules that it exhales, or the impact that the carbon will have on global warming, or the more immediate impact the nimble feline will have on the local songbird populations or... wait, wait, wait. There I go again, tumbling into the maelstrom. The human mind is not built for this. Can't do it, it's impossible. We cannot intellectually understand the web of interconnections related to a single temple cat let alone everything else we might cross paths with on a given day. That level of interconnection is simply too massive for anyone to grasp with their mind.

I can't understand it with my mind but perhaps I can

understand it without my mind. The kind of perception I need is the kind that allows me to walk without calculating the individual firing of every neuron and contraction of every muscle cell that is required for my legs to move under me without falling flat on my face. A bodily understanding.

Being able to see the world with an empty mind is akin to looking at an infrared photo of a familiar scene and realizing that there is a whole new layer of information that you hadn't been aware of. In the case of infrared, it is a flow of heat to and from the things that are there right in front of you yet unseen for lack of the right sensors. Having an empty mind or empty heart would mean being able to see the web of interconnections that underlies all existence as a real and tangible thing. To know the world in its true, essential form. To be enlightened.

I was asked once at a lecture where I had talked about this idea if I thought that I was an enlightened being. The question, of course, was tongue in cheek. I answered it in kind by paraphrasing Mark Twain. "Attaining enlightenment is *easy*," I said, chuckling. "I've done it a thousand times." Twain was talking about quitting cigarettes but the underlying joke is the same. Quitting cigarettes, as with attaining enlightenment, is only meaningful if it sticks, right? But let me ask, of the smokers among us, who doesn't know what it feels like to quit cigarettes again and again? And of those among us who are seeking a true understanding of reality, who hasn't found themselves on the inside edge of awakening more than once?

On an autumn evening, perhaps you are at a gathering of

family and friends with all their individual histories and quirks and arcane relationships, and for a moment, for just a moment, you see it all, the love and loathing, care and neglect, all those streams that intertwine and electrify the room.

On a sunny Sunday, you are at work on your little farm, your veggie patch, and in turning the soil you cut an earthworm in two and realize, too late, that the very soil is alive, and alive in ways you can't even imagine and that what you are eating when you eat those carrots and lettuces is in part the castoff casings of their lives mixed with rain and sunlight and air, and for a moment you sense that you and the worm and the sky and the earth and everything in between are simply extensions of one another.

On a blistering summer day, you dive into an ocean and as the cool water shocks you into alertness, out of nowhere you realize that someone else, at that same instant, has just dived into that same body of water half a world away, or not one but a hundred people, at the very same moment, and they, and you, and all the fish and whales and plankton in the vastness between you are there, in it all together. You sense this, that moment of true awareness, and perhaps for the thousandth time, you find yourself on the cusp of emptiness.

An exquisitely small insect flies over and hovers in front of me, close enough to reveal the fragile details of its little body. A perfect form that appears out of nowhere as if born of the air. I reach out as if to touch it and, in some way, know that I already have.

acknowledgments

Many thanks to Ken Rodgers for his careful reading of the text and to Peter Goodman and all the folks at Stone Bridge Press for their literary skills and constant support.

The tanka poem from the *Man'yōshū* used in "Little Secrets Everywhere" was first published in my book *Songs in the Garden* and was translated from the original Japanese by myself and Kyoko Selden.

ABOUT THE AUTHOR

Marc Peter Keane is a landscape architect, artist, and writer based in Kyōto, Japan, where he has lived for over twenty years. He has published eight books on various topics related to gardens and nature, including the essay collection *The Art of Setting Stones*, the historical design examination *The Japanese Tea Garden*, and the designer's idea book *Japanese Garden Notes*, all from Stone Bridge Press.

Born and raised near New York City, Keane graduated from Cornell University's department of landscape architecture before moving to Kyōto for the first time in the mid 1980s, which then became his home for eighteen years. He opened his own design office in downtown Kyōto, becoming the first foreigner in Japan to receive a working visa as a landscape architect.

Keane's garden design work reflects his background, blending Eastern and Western aesthetics and philosophies. In particular, he has recently been focused on the creation of contemporary *karesansui* gardens (often called Zen gardens in the West) that use traditional Japanese design but express contemporary themes.

More about Keane's work can be found on his website: www. mpkeane.com.